11+
Non-Verbal Reasoning Success

in the 11+ tests

Neil R Williams, Val Mitchell, Sally Moon

Contents

Introduction	About the 11+ tests	4
	Five steps to success	5
	The 11+ Non-verbal reasoning tests	6

1 Find out what you know
	How this book will help you	8
	Where you are now	9
	Taking the test	10
	Marking and summarising the test	11

2 Plan your practice
	Understanding the summary and grid	12
	Non-verbal reasoning grid 1	13

3 Improve your skills

Making connections	Introducing making connections	14
	Common connections	16
	Connections of direction, angle and symmetry	18
	Finding similarities and differences	20
	Spotting distractions	22
Breaking codes	Introducing breaking codes	24
	Codes with two letters	26
	Codes with three letters	28
Finding relationships	Introducing finding relationships	30
	Changing shapes	32
	Number and proportion	34
	Moving and connecting shapes	36
	Reflections in vertical lines	38
	Reflections in horizontal and diagonal lines	40
	Rotations	42
Spotting patterns	Introducing spotting patterns	44
	Simple 2 × 2 grids	46
	More complex 2 × 2 grids	48
	Simple 3 × 3 grids	50
	More complex 3 × 3 grids	52

Contents

Completing sequences	Introducing completing sequences	54
	Repeating patterns	56
	One-step patterns	58
	Two-step patterns	60
	Simple number patterns	62
	Square and triangular number patterns	64

	Non-verbal reasoning essentials	
	Discounting possible answers	66
	Nets of a cube	67
	Working with reflections and rotations	68

4 Test for success	The next steps	70
	Non-verbal reasoning grid 2	71
	Reaching your destination	72
	Non-verbal reasoning connections	73

5 Show what you can do	Preparing for the 11+ tests	74
	Interview techniques	76
	After the tests	78

Test answers	Improve your skills *answers*	79
	Essentials *answers*	81
	Non-verbal reasoning test 1 *answers*	82
	Non-verbal reasoning test 2 *answers*	83

Practice tests	*pull-out section*	
	Non-verbal reasoning test 1	1
	Non-verbal reasoning test 2	7

About the 11+ tests

Introduction

The 11+ tests are used by schools to assess your thinking and learning skills and how you apply these when solving problems in non-verbal and verbal reasoning, maths, comprehension (understanding) and writing.

You will be asked to take a selection of tests that could include some or all of the subjects listed on this page. There are a number of standardised tests schools can use, although some local authorities and schools write their own tests. This book guides you through the question styles, formats and levels of difficulty in the standardised tests, as well as providing examples of other question types that frequently occur.

Schools will often give you an interview in addition to the tests so that they can find out more about you. They may also set a problem-solving task.

Subjects set in the 11+ tests

Non-verbal reasoning
Non-verbal reasoning tests ask you to solve puzzles and problems that involve visual patterns or sequences and their connections.

Verbal reasoning
Verbal reasoning tests ask you to solve puzzles and problems that involve letters, words and numbers and the connections between them.

Maths
The Maths paper will consist of a written test and probably a mental maths test in which the questions are read out to you. Calculators are not allowed in either test. Schools often write their own mental maths tests. The papers generally test the following skills.

Main test
- Numbers and their properties
- Calculations (including algebra)
- Fractions, decimals and percentages
- Working with charts and data
- Shape and space
- Measuring
- Data handling

Mental maths test

English
The English paper will consist of a reading test and may also contain a separate writing task. There is no standardised form of writing task and schools often create their own. The papers are generally divided in the following ways.

Reading
- Comprehension
- Grammar
- Punctuation
- Spelling

Writing

Essential research

- Find out as much information as possible about your selected schools well in advance.
- You can find information on dates and entrance exams for state grammar schools on your local authority website or the school website.
- Individual schools include information in their prospectuses and additional information is often available on the school websites or at open days.
- Closing dates for applications vary, so you should check these well in advance.

Introduction

Five steps to success

11+ Non-Verbal Reasoning Success is designed to help you prepare for the 11+ Non-verbal reasoning paper in **five simple steps** so that you can take the tests with confidence.

The colour-coded sections in this guide split up the process, making it easy to follow.

1 Test — Find out what you know

Take Test 1 in the centre of the book and mark your answers. This will show what you already know and where you need to do more work.

2 Track — Plan your practice

Fill in the grids to target the specific skills you want to develop. This will help you to plan your work and decide how much time you need to set aside.

3 Teach — Improve your skills

Work through the Skills pages indicated by your grids and test yourself with the questions at the end of each section. All the answers are clearly explained to help you understand where you have gone wrong if you make any mistakes. Colour in the progress chart.

4 Test — Test for success

Take Test 2 in the centre of the book and mark your scores on the second set of grids to find out how you have improved.

Missed a few skills? Don't worry, just go back through any of the Skills pages you need to work on…

You can now move on to a full 11+ test, fully prepared. Look at the list of papers available on the inside front cover to see which is most suitable for you.

5 Present — Show what you can do

Practise your presentation skills using the interview tips and techniques on pages 76–77. If you are asked for an interview at the school you have chosen, this is your chance to shine.

Introduction

The 11+ Non-verbal reasoning tests are designed to test your ability to solve problems that have visual images, patterns and grids.

You may be required to take a Non-verbal reasoning test in addition to Maths and English. Although there is no curriculum to follow, there are a number of skills that are tested which you will be familiar with.

Non-verbal reasoning test

Making connections

The skills covered

This section will include a range of questions that test your skills in making connections between a series of images.

What you will have to do

You will be asked questions to see if you can…

- find connections related to…
  - shape
  - size
  - shading
  - number of shapes
  - position
  - variety of shapes
  - angles
- work with the connections to identify differences and similarities
- pick out any distracting images that might be there to trick you.

Breaking codes

The skills covered

This section will include a range of questions that test your skills in breaking a visual code that is linked to two or three letters. To break each code you must identify which part of the image is represented by which letter.

What you will have to do

You will be asked questions to see if you can…

- identify which part of the image is represented by which letter
- identify common connections between images
- find a rule and apply it in new situations.

Finding relationships

The skills covered

This section will include a range of questions that test your skills in spotting how images are linked together in different ways.

What you will have to do

You will be asked questions to see if you understand…

- how to find different relationships between images
- how to compare different types of reflection
- how to identify rotation and translation
- how to apply relationships to a shape
- how to predict what comes next.

Introduction

Spotting patterns

The skills covered

This section will include a range of questions that test your skills in picking out patterns in grid layouts. You will also be expected to identify patterns and use them to complete each grid.

What you will have to do

You will be asked questions to see if you can…

- spot patterns in grid questions
- work logically to solve the problem
- apply changes from one image to another.

How to complete sequences

The skills covered

This section will include a range of questions that test whether you can pick out the differences between images, even when they are partially hidden.

What you will have to do

You will be asked questions to see if you can…

- spot repeating patterns
- check for one-step patterns
- check for more complex number patterns
- use numbers to complete a sequence
- complete logical visual sequences.

SATs practice

Although non-verbal reasoning is not taught in schools, you will find that maths skills relating to Knowing and using number facts and Understanding shape are helpful in solving non-verbal reasoning problems. Many of the skills you will learn in Chapter 3 *Improve your skills* relate to these areas of Maths and practising these will help you in your SATs preparations.

INTERVIEWS

Schools often make their final selection by interviewing the candidates. This is where you get a chance to show your potential to be a good member of the school, and to find out whether this is the right place for you. Find out about more about interview techniques on pages 76–77.

The 11+ Non-verbal reasoning tests

1 Find out what you know

This book is designed to help you succeed in your 11+ Non-verbal reasoning tests. After you have taken the first Practice test in the pull-out booklet, you will be directed to the appropriate *Improve your skills* pages in Chapter 3. After completing these pages, use the second more challenging Practice test to check you are ready for the 11+ tests.

The final chapter in the book, *5 Show what you can do*, will help you to build your confidence as the 11+ tests approach and prepare you for the interview that many schools give.

Understanding the skills

After taking the first Practice test, Chapter *3 Improve your skills* will...

- help you to find ways of identifying the **connections** between images and how to spot distractions
- show you methods for **breaking codes** in a logical and methodical way
- demonstrate techniques for **spotting patterns** and applying these patterns in new situations
- help you to understand how to **find relationships** between different images through comparison and reflection.

Practising the skills

To help you practise these skills as you work through the book, you will find…

- example questions and a short test in each section, providing extra practice
- 'Try it out' activities to build your skills
- tips for how to solve problems and practise the skills in different ways.

Preparing for the tests

When your practice is complete, Chapter *5 Show what you can do* on pages 74–77 can help you to relax and prepare yourself in the final week. It contains…

- a range of activities to do with your parents and friends to help you become more familiar with the skills you have learnt
- a 'countdown' list to help you get ready
- interview advice on how to dress, relax and communicate
- information about what happens after you get your 11+ test results.

1 Find out what you know

Where you are now

Before you begin your 11+ practice, you need to work out how much you already know. As well as using this book, you may find it helpful to ask your school or your tutor about the skills you need to work on. The Internet is another useful source of information.

Non-verbal reasoning is not tested in SATs (the Statutory Assessment Tests) but the skills involved in answering many of the questions are covered in the **Understanding shape** and **Knowing and using number facts** learning objectives of the Primary Framework for Mathematics.

Teacher's assessment

Teachers assess your progress during the year in Maths. This assessment is often scored in thirds of a Level: 2c, 2b, 2a; 3c, 3b, 3a; 4c, 4b, 4a; 5c, 5b, 5a. An 'a' score is the highest in each Level.

Your school may predict the Level you will reach in Maths at the end of each Key Stage and you can ask for these records.

Tutors

If you are using an independent tutor or tuition school, they will have similar information to your own school. Ask them if they hold a record of your Non-verbal reasoning and Verbal reasoning abilities.

Maths skills

Understanding shape

Making sure that you can identify shapes and angles will help you with Non-verbal reasoning.

Complete the chart below to check that you can identify 2-D shapes and understand their properties, including lines of symmetry, reflection and rotation.

Angles

Understanding the different types of angle can help you to identify the rotation of images. Fill in the table to help you remember them.

Degrees	Angle name
0–89	A_____
90	R_____
90–180	O_____
180–360	R_____

Knowing and using number facts

Having an understanding of common number sequences such as multiples, square numbers, cube numbers and triangular numbers can be helpful when working with questions involving number sequences. These are given in the form of shapes to count within boxes rather than numbers on a page.

Number of sides	Shape name	Properties of the shape
1	a Circle b Oval/ ellipse	a is a regular shape with an infinite number of lines of symmetry b is regular shape with two lines of symmetry and rotational order 2
2		
3		
4		
5		
6		
7		

1 Find out what you know

Now you are ready to take the first Practice test in the pull-out booklet, it is important to make sure you have the right conditions to get an accurate result.

This Practice test will help you to identify the areas you will need to target to improve your skills before taking the 11+ Non-verbal reasoning test.

Timing

It is better to do the test in the morning at a weekend when you are at your best, rather than after school when you have had a long day.

Allow 45 minutes to take the test plus at least half an hour to get everything organised.

Equipment

You should have the following items assembled before you begin:
- pen • pencil • eraser
- pencil sharpener • ruler
- timer (this can be the timer on an oven or an alarm clock)
- analogue watch/clock (as this will help you to see how much time you've got left)
- paper (for jotting ideas and your start and finish times)
- tracing paper and a small mirror (to help with reflection and rotation questions).

Surroundings

Use a clear table or desk where you can set out the materials you will be using. Make sure the area is quiet and without any distractions.

TIPS FOR SUCCESS

- Read each question twice.
- Check carefully what you are being asked to look for.
- Don't guess any answers even if you are short of time. These tests are to help you find out areas where you need practice.

Question types

Multiple-choice

If you are taking a 'standardised' 11+ Non-verbal reasoning test, you can expect this to be in a multiple-choice format set out in different styles by section. You may have a separate booklet to mark your answers in.

Questions with images

Many of the questions will have a selection of images to choose from linked to a list of letter options (usually A to E). These letters are also printed in the answer booklet when one is provided, and you simply mark the answer against the letter as instructed. You will find a lot of questions laid out in this style in the non-verbal reasoning tests in this book. These will help you become familiar with this type of question. Always complete them in the way you are instructed.

Questions with letter codes

A number of other questions in the standardised tests (where an answer booklet is supplied) provide you with a series of two- or three-letter codes. Each letter in the code represents an element from the images provided. Match the answer option to the new image and mark the answer booklet as instructed.

Written format

When local authorities, schools and examination boards set their own papers, you are more likely to be asked to write your answer down than fill in a booklet. You may occasionally be asked to draw the missing image.

1 Find out what you know

Once you have completed the first Practice test in the pull-out booklet, you will be ready to mark it and review your results. Do this by following the stages below.

Marking

- Go to the *Answers* on page 82. Score your completed paper by filling in the blank boxes in the 'Mark*' column. There is one mark allowed for each complete question. **There are no half marks**.

- Now turn to *Non-verbal reasoning grid 1* on page 13.

- Transfer your marks to the 'Mark*' column.

- Add up the total for each section.

- Add up the total for all the sections in the final box at the end of the Non-verbal reasoning grid 1.

- Work out the percentage as directed in the Summary box below.

Non-verbal reasoning grid 1

2 Plan your practice

Follow the instructions on page 11 to fill in this grid and page 12 for instructions for use.

Making connections

Question	Mark*	Skill	Page	To do	Try it out	Test yourself
1	/	Common connections	16			
2	/	Connections of direction, angle and symmetry	18			
3	/					
4	/	Finding similarities and differences	20			
5	/	Spotting distractions	22			
6						
Total	1 /6 5	Read 'Introducing making connections' first on pages 14–15 if you have missed any Skills in the Making connections section.				

Breaking codes

Question	Mark*	Skill	Page	To do	Try it out	Test yourself
7	/					
8	/	Codes with two letters	26			
9	/					
10	/	Codes with three letters	28			
11	/					
Total	/ 5 5	Read 'Introducing breaking codes' first on pages 24–25 if you have missed any Skills in the Breaking codes section.				

Finding relationships

Question	Mark*	Skill	Page	To do	Try it out	Test yourself
12						
13		Changing shapes	32			
14		Number and proportion	34			
15						
16		Moving and connecting shapes	36			
17						
18		Reflections in vertical lines**	38			
19		Reflections in horizontal and diagonal lines**	40			
20						
21		Rotations**	42			
Total	8/10	Read 'Introducing finding relationships' first on pages 30–31 if you have missed any skills in the Finding relationships section.				

** If you find these skills challenging, try the extra practice questions in 'Working with reflections and rotations' on pages 68–69.

Spotting patterns

Question	Mark*	Skill	Page	To do	Try it out	Test yourself
22		Simple 2 × 2 grids	46			
23		More complex 2 × 2 grids	48			
24		Simple 3 × 3 grids	50			
25		More complex 3 × 3 grids	52			
26						
Total	4 /5	Read 'Introducing spotting patterns' first on pages 44–45 if you have missed any skills in the Spotting patterns section.				

Completing sequences

Question	Mark*	Skill	Page	To do	Try it out	Test yourself
27	/	Repeating patterns	56			
28	/					
29	/	One-step patterns	58			
30	/					
31	/	Two-step patterns	60			
32	/					
33	/	Simple number patterns (if you miss this skill, you should also practise 'Square and triangular number patterns' below)	62			
34	/	Square and triangular number patterns	64			
Total	8 /8	Read 'Introducing completing sequences' first on pages 54–55 if you have missed any Skills in the Completing sequences section.				

*1 mark is allocated for each correct answer. There are no half marks.

| Total | 30 /34 | Add up your total for your Non-verbal reasoning test here. |

Non-verbal reasoning test 1 summary

Total ☐

Percentage ☐

Work out your percentage using this sum

$\dfrac{\text{Total}}{34} \times 100 =$

2 Plan your practice

The summary and grid on this page are essential tools in helping you plan your 11+ practice. Refer to the summary for a guide to the time you will need to set aside, and the grid to work out which skills you will need to practise.

Reviewing the summary

Your summary score on page 11 will give you an idea of how much time you will need to set aside for your 11+ practice.

Refer to the list below to get an overview of your abilities in non-verbal reasoning.

Up to 40%   You may need to plan 9–12 months of practice before attempting the 11+.

41–50%   Feel encouraged that you will benefit from this book, although you may need to work through most of the skills pages.

51–70%   You have many skills that will help you in your 11+ tests already and will benefit from the support this book will give you.

71–100%   When you are confident in working with the targeted skills, move on to the second (harder) Practice test in the pull-out booklet.

Understanding the grid

The Non-verbal reasoning grid, opposite, is an essential tool in planning your 11+ practice.

Look at the 'To do' column on the grid. You will see that the questions are grouped into blocks.

- Colour the blocks in **green** where you have answered all the questions **right**.
- Colour the blocks in **red** where you have answered any of the questions **wrong**.

Red sections

Look at the sections (Making connections, Breaking codes, Finding relationships, Spotting patterns and Completing sequences) where you have coloured blocks in red.

Begin by reading the relevant Introductions to these sections in Chapter *3 Improve your skills* (the page numbers are written next to the headings). For example, if you have coloured 'Common connections' in red, then you should begin by reading *'Introducing making connections'* on page 14.

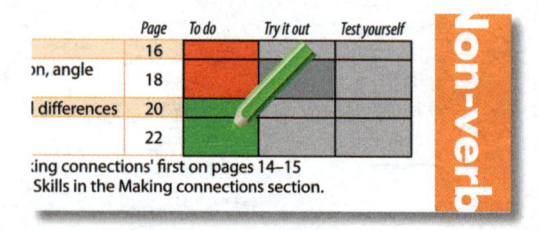

Now work through the rest of the section in *3 Improve your skills* to complete the skills you marked in red earlier.

- Read through the text.
- Have a go at the 'Try it out' activities.
- Complete the questions at the end and check your answers on pages 79–80.
- When you have finished the skill, colour in the 'Try it out' and 'Test yourself' boxes on Non-verbal reasoning grid 1.

Make a note of any questions you found difficult so that you can go back to these pages again before you take the 11+ test.

Green sections

If you have coloured any blocks in green, you have already mastered some of the easier skills needed in these sections, so you may not want to go through them as thoroughly. However, skimming quickly through the pages and trying out some activities will provide you with some tips to help you to speed up your test technique and tackle more difficult questions.

Working through the questions on these pages will also help to build your confidence in areas that you enjoy.

2 Plan your practice

Non-verbal reasoning grid 1

Follow the instructions on page 11 to fill in this grid and page 12 for instructions for use.

Making connections

Question	Mark*	Skill	Page	To do	Try it out	Test yourself
1		Common connections	16		▓	
2		Connections of direction, angle and symmetry	18		▓	
3					▓	
4		Finding similarities and differences	20			
5		Spotting distractions	22			
6						
Total	/6	Read 'Introducing making connections' first on pages 14–15 if you have missed any Skills in the Making connections section.				

Breaking codes

Question	Mark*	Skill	Page	To do	Try it out	Test yourself
7		Codes with two letters	26		▓	
8					▓	
9					▓	
10		Codes with three letters	28		▓	
11					▓	
Total	/5	Read 'Introducing breaking codes' first on pages 24–25 if you have missed any Skills in the Breaking codes section.				

Finding relationships

Question	Mark*	Skill	Page	To do	Try it out	Test yourself
12		Changing shapes	32			
13						
14		Number and proportion	34		▓	
15					▓	
16		Moving and connecting shapes	36			
17						
18		Reflections in vertical lines**	38			
19		Reflections in horizontal and diagonal lines**	40			
20		Rotations**	42			
21						
Total	/10	Read 'Introducing finding relationships' first on pages 30–31 if you have missed any skills in the Finding relationships section.				

** If you find these skills challenging, try the extra practice questions in 'Working with reflections and rotations' on pages 68–69.

Spotting patterns

Question	Mark*	Skill	Page	To do	Try it out	Test yourself
22		Simple 2 × 2 grids	46			
23		More complex 2 × 2 grids	48		▓	
24		Simple 3 × 3 grids	50		▓	
25		More complex 3 × 3 grids	52			
26						
Total	/5	Read 'Introducing spotting patterns' first on pages 44–45 if you have missed any skills in the Spotting patterns section.				

Completing sequences

Question	Mark*	Skill	Page	To do	Try it out	Test yourself
27		Repeating patterns	56			
28						
29		One-step patterns	58			
30						
31		Two-step patterns	60			
32						
33		Simple number patterns (if you miss this skill, you should also practise 'Square and triangular number patterns' below)	62			
34						
	▓	Square and triangular number patterns	64			
Total	/8	Read 'Introducing completing sequences' first on pages 54–55 if you have missed any Skills in the Completing sequences section.				

*1 mark is allocated for each correct answer. There are no half marks.

Total /34 Add up your total for your Non-verbal reasoning test here.

13

3 Improve your skills

Non-verbal reasoning is all about *making connections* between small images. Sometimes you'll find there is only one connection, but when there are lots of connections you'll need to sort out which ones are relevant.

The trick to finding the connections between these images is to know what sort of similarities and changes to look out for. Non-verbal reasoning tests don't need you to remember lots of facts. Just observe what is happening and work out what should go with the images you are given.

What to expect

There are lots of small ways that images can be changed. Within making connections you'll see a wide range of similarities including…

| shape | size | shading | number of shapes |
| position | variety of shapes | angles |

In making connections you'll look at each type of connection individually. When you combine two or more connections, you start to build relationships between the shapes.

Sometimes questions will seem to show a connection that doesn't quite seem to fit. These are known as 'distractions'. They are there to make the questions a little bit harder, so you'll look at how to spot them.

Useful word skills

Box
Many of the questions you will see in non-verbal reasoning put the images inside square boxes. The word **box** is used for that container. As squares can be used in the questions, the book refers to **square** for the shape and box for the container.

Clockwise and anticlockwise
To work with rotations of shapes it will be useful to know clockwise from anticlockwise. Clockwise is the direction that a hand goes around the clock, from one to two…to twelve. Anticlockwise is when it goes from twelve to eleven…to one.

Regular shapes
Regular shapes are shapes where every angle is the same and every side has the same length. Squares and equilateral triangles are two examples of regular shapes. A circle is also a regular shape, despite it not having any straight sides.

Irregular shapes
Irregular shapes are shapes that have different angles or sides of different length. A rectangle is irregular as not all the sides are the same length, despite all the angles being the same.

14

Making connections

Skills in understanding connections

A **connection** is something that is similar about the images you are looking at. You can use connections to compare the images.

- The first shape is a black triangle and the second shape is a black circle.
- Both shapes are regular.

The 'colour' is clearly a connection between the two images. If you were looking at a question that asked you to pick a 'shape' that could be grouped with these two, you'd be looking for a shape that was black.

Note also that both shapes are 'regular'. This is useful information, especially if there are two black shapes to pick from.

Spotting the connections is an important skill, but being able to spot what changes is equally important. Putting the connections and the changes together will lead you to the answer.

- What is happening in this example?

You can see that the 'shape' itself is the only thing that changes.

Question type skills

Odd one out

In these questions you'll be shown five images and asked to pick the one that doesn't really belong with the others.

Most like

In these questions you'll be shown two images that are part of a 'set'. You'll then be asked to pick one from a group of five that should also be part of the set.

What you will learn

In this section you will learn:

- the most common connections

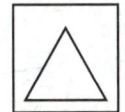

- what the changes can look like

- some of the common distractions used in questions.

TIPS FOR SUCCESS

Be prepared

- Finding the connections is not too difficult, but there are some things you can do to help yourself.
- Make sure your eyes are rested – you'll be looking at lots of small images and tired eyes will make it harder.
- If you wear glasses, make sure you clean them before the test so that you have the clearest view possible.

15

3 Improve your skills

You will see many *common connections* in non-verbal reasoning questions. Generally you'll find it's easy to spot one or two connections between a pair of images.

Whenever you are looking at non-verbal reasoning questions just take it one step at a time. Look for anything that seems to remain the same and anything that seems to change consistently.

Understanding common connections

Here is the first set of common connections to think about:

   line style   shape   shading   size

Shape can mean a regular shape that is being moved around or a series of irregular shapes with the same number of lines.

Shading can be black, white or anything in between, with a variety of patterns.

When it comes to thinking about size, it's a good idea to think about the Russian wooden dolls that fit inside each other. They are often precisely painted but always in proportion to each other.

Skills in line style connections

Solid lines

Solid lines are the most common type of line you will see. Generally, any shape that isn't white will have a solid line as it would be too difficult to spot the pattern in the line against the shading of the shape. Sometimes the lines can be of different thicknesses.

Dashed lines

The lines of shapes, or even arrows, can have different patterns to them, just like the white lines down the middle of a road.

Shape skills

Regular shapes

Regular shapes look more familiar and this can make them easier, even though the connections you'll find are generally the same as those for the irregular shapes.

- What connections can you find between these two shapes?

  Both shapes have 'dashed lines' around the outside and the dashes are the 'same length'. They have 'no shading' on the inside. They are both 'regular' shapes: one is a square and the other is a pentagon.

Irregular shapes

Irregular shapes can be trickier than regular shapes as you know more about regular shapes.

Some irregular shapes will have the same number of corners or the same number of straight lines.

- Have a look at these two shapes and see if you can spot anything else that connects them.

  Both shapes have 'solid lines' around the outside and have 'no shading' on the inside. They both have nine 'corners'.

Making connections

Skills in shading connections

Simple shading
Non-verbal reasoning tests are printed in black and white. The simplest shading is solid black or solid white, which is sometimes seen as no shading.

Patterned shading
Shading patterns are used to give variety to the shading, as colour can't be used. Some patterns are striped – vertical, horizontally or diagonally. The diagonal shading will always be at an angle of 45°, but could be going up or down. Some patterns are spotted, with different sized spots and different sized gaps between them. Other patterns are chequered and some are like grid lines.

- Look at the different shading patterns shown here.

Changing from one type of shading to another is one of the most common changes you'll see in questions. When questions have more connections in them you may see as many as four different types of shading.

Skills in size connections

Enlargements and reductions
Another common change is in size. The shapes can be made bigger or smaller but still stay the same shape, just like these two circles. You are more likely to see this sort of change in a regular shape than an irregular one.

TRY IT OUT

Odd one out
Here's a game to play with a few friends:

- Gather together a group of objects that are linked together in some way.
- Add an item that looks like it could be part of the group but doesn't quite fit.
- See if your friends can work out the object that isn't part of the group and the reason why.
- Award one point for choosing the correct object and one for the correct reason.
- Your friends will need to bring their own groups of objects.
- Who can get the highest score?

Common connections

TEST YOURSELF

Look at the five shapes in each row. What connects *four* of the shapes and makes the other shape the odd one out? Circle the letter under the shape that you think is most *unlike* the others.

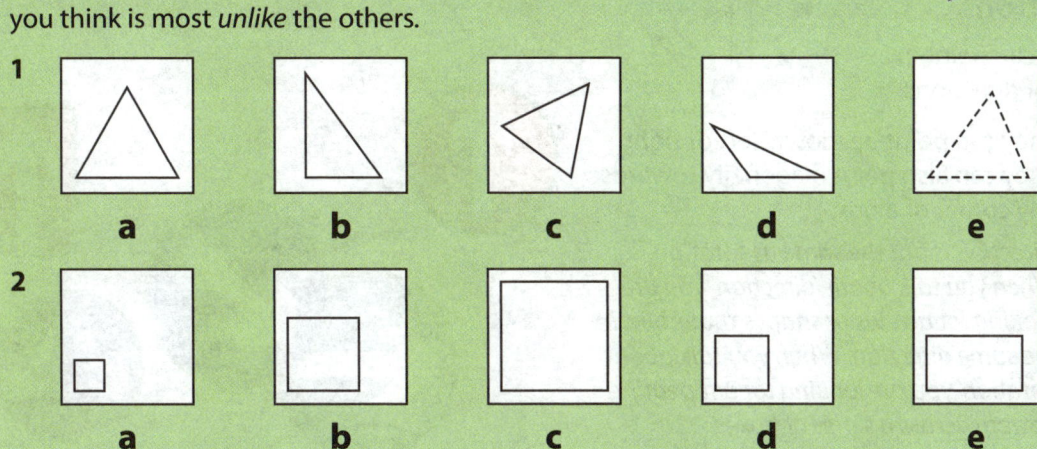

1. a   b   c   d   e

2. a   b   c   d   e

17

3 Improve your skills

Understanding more complex connections

Here is a second set of common connections for you to think about:

arrows **direction** **angles** **symmetry**

Arrows and directions are often linked together, and that's how you'll look at them on this page.

When you look at angles it is worth remembering that an acute angle is less than 90°, a right angle is exactly 90°, an obtuse angle is between 90° and 180°, and a reflex angle is more than 180°.

Skills in arrow connections

Arrow heads

Arrows are used in some question types more than others, but wherever they are used there are a couple of things that can be changed. The first is the design of the arrow head.

- Look at the four arrows and see how the arrow heads have changed.

  One is a simple triangle, one is just two lines, the third is a triangle with a curved base and the last is a diamond.

  Remember that arrows can point in various directions, so some of the arrow heads may look different because the arrows are shown at unusual angles.

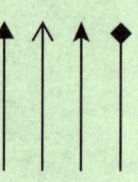

Arrow tails

Robin Hood's arrows always had decent tails on them – the tail ensured that the arrow would go where it was meant to. The tail can be another important connection.

- Have a look at these three arrows with identical heads.

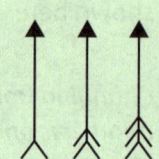

  Each arrow has a different number of tail 'fins'. The first has one, the second has two and the third has three. You should count each pair of lines as one fin.

  Generally the fins will point in the same direction as the head.

Direction

Arrows can point in a range of directions.

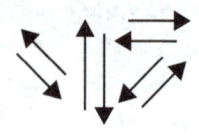

- They can point up, down, left or right. They can also point diagonally towards any corner of a box.

  Direction is not the same as rotation. When you talk about 'direction' you are looking for arrows or shapes that point in the same direction. When you talk about 'rotation' you are looking for a repeating pattern across a series of boxes.

Connections of direction, angle and symmetry

18

Making connections

Skills in angle connections
Angle types

Sometimes you can look at a question and struggle to spot the connections, especially when the question is about angle as it's not something you'll generally think about. Shading is much more obvious as it's more visual.

- Look at the three triangles. One triangle has a right angle and one has an obtuse angle, but at first glance they are just triangles.

  In angle questions the connection might be that all the shapes have a right angle or an obtuse angle. It could also be that the angles with a connection are acute.

Skills in symmetry connections
Shapes

Probably the least common of the common connections is 'symmetry'. The shapes may 'share' a line of symmetry or have their own line of symmetry.

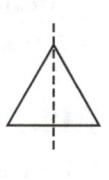

Patterns

In some questions each box will contain a number of shapes and a line of symmetry will go 'through' the box.

- Look at this box containing four shapes.

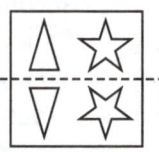

  This example has a 'horizontal' line of symmetry.

TIPS FOR SUCCESS
Do the twist

Spotting right angles can be tricky if the lines making the right angle are not horizontal and vertical, as that's what you are used to looking for. If you suspect that an angle is a right angle, make one of the lines horizontal either by angling your head or turning the paper round. If the other line is vertical then you know you've got a right angle.

If that doesn't help you can try using the corner of a sheet of plain paper to see if the angle is a right angle.

TEST YOURSELF

The two shapes on the left are part of a set. Which of the five shapes on the right belongs with the set? Circle the letter under the shape that you think is the correct answer.

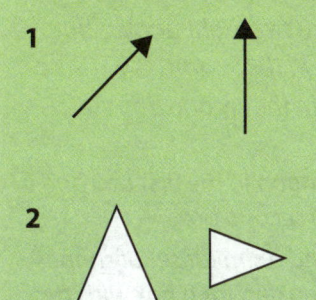

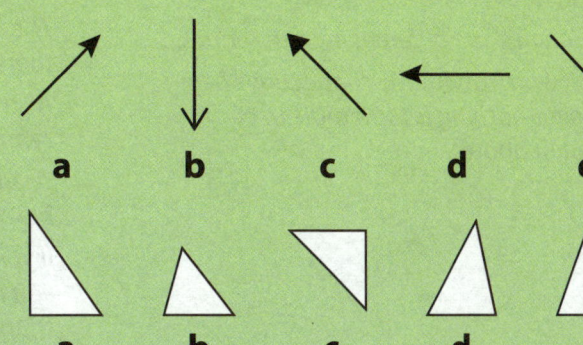

1.   a   b   c   d   e

2.   a   b   c   d   e

Connections of direction, angle and symmetry

19

3 Improve your skills

One way of *making connections* is to find similarities and differences.

Sometimes you are asked to make connections between single shapes, sometimes between groups of shapes.

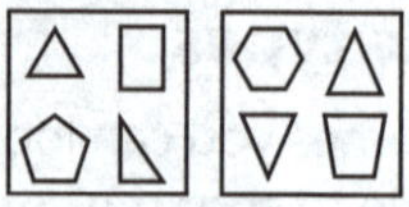

Understanding similarities and differences

Here are some common connections that may be found:

line style	shape	shading	size
arrows	direction	angles	symmetry

You will not see every possible connection in one question, but you could see two or three different ones.

Most connections will be relevant, but there will be some that are not. An irrelevant connection is a **distraction** and will be looked at on pages 22–23.

Sometimes finding the differences can be like a game of 'spot the difference', so keep your eyes open for any changes that may be there.

Skills in working with simple images

Single shapes

Questions with single shapes are usually the easiest as there are only a few possible connections.

- Have a look at these two single shapes and see what connections you can find that are the **same**.

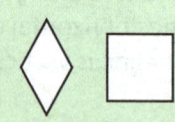

  Both shapes have four 'sides'.
  Both shapes have 'solid lines'.
  Both shapes are 'white'.

- Now look again and see if you can find the **differences**:

  The first 'shape' is a diamond, the second is a square.
  The 'angles' are different in both shapes.
  Don't worry about the connections being simple – nothing is too simple to be thought about.

Small groups of shapes

Small groups of shapes can also have connections.

- What **similarities** can you find between these two boxes?

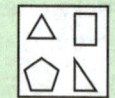

  Both boxes have four 'shapes'.
  Both boxes have two 'triangles'.
  Both boxes have a 'quadrilateral'.
  All the shapes are unshaded outlines.

- What about the **differences**?

  There are 15 'corners' in the first box, but 16 in the second box.
  The first box has five 'right angles', but there are none in the second box.
  All the shapes in the second box are symmetrical.
  There is a pentagon in the first box and a hexagon in the second box.
  If you had to find a similar set of shapes you might be looking for a box with two triangles, a quadrilateral and one more shape, all of which are white.

Making connections

Skills in working with complex images

Segmented shapes

Segmented shapes are usually regular shapes that have been split into various pieces or segments. They will often be connected by shading.

- Have a look at these two shapes and see if you can spot the **connections**.

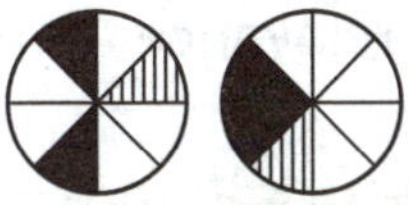

  Both shapes are split into eight 'equal' segments.

  The 'lines' for the segments seem to be in the same place.

  Each shape has two segments 'shaded black'.

  Each shape has one segment which has 'vertical striped shading'.

- Are there any **differences**?

  In the first shape the shaded sections are all separate, but in the second shape they are all together.

  This difference is quite useful. Often this sort of shape will be used in 'rotation' questions, but as the gaps between the shaded segments have gone you know that's not the case. Rotation questions are covered on pages 42–43.

Compound shapes

Compound shapes are made up of several shapes and often look like something you would recognise.

- This compound shape looks like a rather old car.

  With compound shapes there can be lots of connections as each little shape can have connections of its own. For now it is useful to be aware of compound shapes, but they are looked at in more detail on page 45.

TRY IT OUT
Leaves

The next time you are out for a walk, collect some leaves which are different shapes, sizes and colours.

- Take a pair of leaves and compare them.
- How are they similar?
- How are they different?
- Are there any common patterns between the leaves?
- This sort of activity will help you spot connections more quickly.

TEST YOURSELF

The two images on the left are part of a set. Which of the five images on the right belongs with the set? Circle the letter under the image that you think is the correct answer.

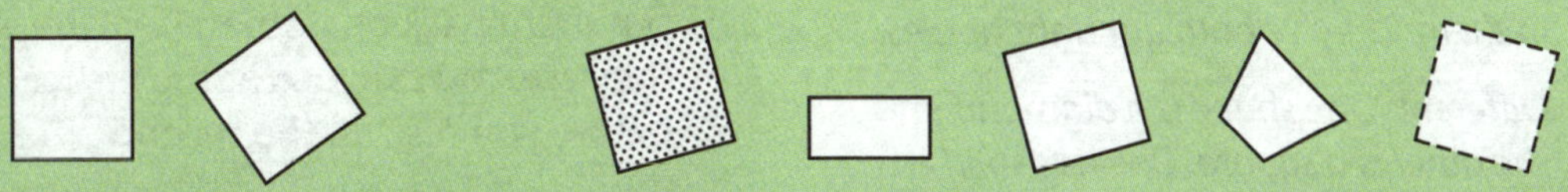

1

a b c d e

2

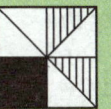

a b c d e

Finding similarities and differences

21

3 Improve your skills

Spotting distractions

Not every connection is part of the question. *Spotting distractions* is all about finding the connections that are there to confuse you.

In word puzzles in maths you often have to sort out what is important and what is nonsense. Sometimes you'll find that connections have been put in that don't have any relevance to the question.

Understanding distractions

Any connector can be a distraction but the most common ones are…

- extra shapes
- compound shapes
- shading
- combination of shapes
- arrows

When you find something that is a distraction, it can unlock a question. Knowing that you can ignore the distraction helps you to focus on the important connections.

Distractions appear everywhere in the world. How many times have you not paid attention to what your teacher has been saying because you've been fiddling with a pencil or a ruler?

Skills in spotting distractions

One step at a time

In some questions it's obvious that something is not relevant. If it's different in every image it's probably not going to be relevant.

- Have a look at these two shapes and describe what is the same and what is different about the shapes.

Same: The shapes are both quadrilaterals with solid lines around the outside and some sort of shading in them. They've both got right angles.

Different: One shape is a diamond and the other is a square. One has solid black shading while the other has stripes.

In these two shapes the shading or the rotation could be the distraction, but you can't be certain until you've also looked at the possible answers.

TRY IT OUT
Concentrate

Everyone gets distracted, but different people get distracted by different things. Can you concentrate for long enough to complete this challenge?

- Take a pack of playing cards and use all of the aces, twos, threes, fours, fives and sixes.
- Shuffle the 24 cards and then place them all face down on a table.
- Pick up two cards at a time. If the colour and the number match you can put them to the side. If they don't just put them back but remember where they are. You can look at the first card before you pick up the second.
- How many goes do you need to get all 12 pairs?
- How many more goes do you need if you use the full pack of 52 cards?

Making connections

Spotting distractions

Using the whole question

1 Distractions can be tricky to spot, especially if you've only got two images to look at. You can often get clues from the five possible answers you are given.

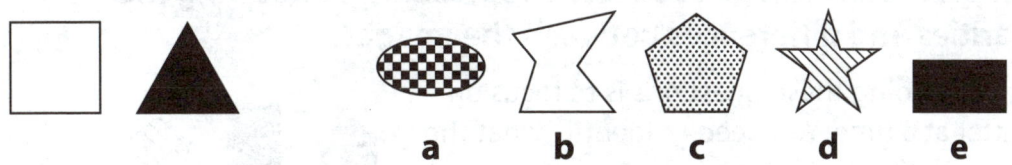

- Which of the shapes on the right should be with the two on the left?

  Start by looking at the similarities and the differences:

  Same: The two shapes have straight lines. They are both regular shapes.

  Different: The two shapes have a different number of corners and different shading.

  *Now look at the five possible answers. Four of them have straight lines but only **c** is a regular shape and that's the correct answer. If you look at the shading you can see it was a distraction. The patterns were not relevant to the question.*

2 Here's another example to look at.

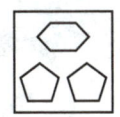

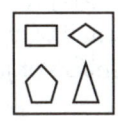

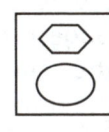

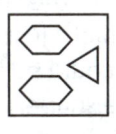

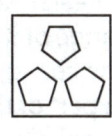

- What is the same and what is different about the two boxes on the left?

  Same: They both have one hexagon in them. All of the shapes have solid lines and no shading. The shapes in both boxes have 16 corners.

  Different: The first box has two shapes, the second one has three shapes.

The combination of shapes in the box is not going to be relevant, but the hexagon or the number of corners will be.

- Hexagon: Boxes **b**, **c** and **e** have at least one hexagon in them.
- Corners: Box **a** has 16 corners, **b** has 6, **c** has 15, **d** has 15 and **e** has 12.

  *Both **b** and **e** have one hexagon, but the number of corners is different.*
  *If the hexagon and just straight lines are the deciding factors it could be **e**.*
  *If the number of corners is important the answer has to be **a**.*

  *In this example the answer is **a**. The hexagon itself was the distraction in this question.*

TEST YOURSELF

The two boxes on the left are part of a set. Which of the five boxes on the right belongs with the set? Circle the letter under the box that you think is the correct answer.

3 Improve your skills

Code-breaking questions consist of a series of images, each with a two- or three-letter code. To break the code you must identify which part of the image each letter represents by spotting the similarities and differences between the images.

The trick to doing these questions is to focus on one letter at a time. You need to identify what the images with that letter have in common.

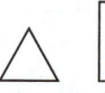

AQ   CQ   AP   BR   ?

What to expect

Features of the images that might change in questions on breaking codes include:

shape   size   shading/patterns   number of shapes
orientation   combination of shapes

The feature that each part of the code represents might completely change or it might just change in a small way. For example, the change could be to the entire shape or just to the shading on part of the shape.

Breaking codes skills

When you tackle this skill in the 11+ test, you will be asked to look at codes with two or even three letters. The examples here show how to start by looking at one letter only to help you to build this skill.

Spotting changes in shape

1 Look for differences between the shapes.

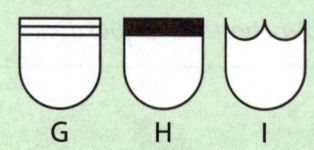

G   H   I

- These three shield shapes are all different, but can you see what the differences are?

    G has some horizontal lines at the top.

    H has a black stripe at the top.

    I has three points at the top.

2 Now that you know what the differences are, look for what doesn't change.

- What stays the same in the three shield shapes?

    The height of all three shields is the same.

    The width of all three shields is the same.

    The main colour of all three shields is the same.

    The curve at the bottom of all three shields is the same – sometimes you may see this replaced with an angle.

It's always useful to know what stays the same as sometimes that can be used to distract you.

Introducing breaking codes

Breaking codes

Combinations of shapes

It is possible that in a question, two shapes will be put together as one item.

- What are the shape combinations shown here?

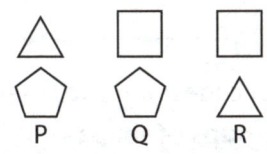

  P   Q   R

  P has a triangle and a pentagon.

  Q has a square and a pentagon.

  R has a square and a triangle.

  This is a bit of a distraction, so if you find it hard to work out what's going on with some shapes, see if they work together as a group.

Shading

Shading is one of the most common changes you'll see. Often you'll be given white, black and a pattern, but sometimes you'll get two patterns with either white or black.

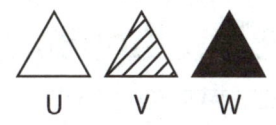

U   V   W

- What are the shading changes shown here?

  U is solid white.

  V has a striped pattern.

  W is solid black.

  Some questions will put two different shading patterns together so the outer shape has one type of shading and an inner shape has a different type. You'll see some of these examples on the next few pages.

TIPS FOR SUCCESS

You can use words

As the codes get more complicated, it can be tricky to remember what each letter means. Although it's a 'non-verbal' test, you can write down words on the paper to help jog your memory. Remember to keep it simple. Something like G = lines is usually enough.

For differences in shading, you can scribble a small box with the type of shading or pattern for a particular letter.

What you will learn

In this section you will learn how to:

- identify differences between symbols
- identify common connectors between symbols
- find a rule and apply it
- break two- and three-letter codes.

TRY IT OUT

Distraction

Play a game with your friends to see who is the quickest to spot a pattern in some plastic containers.

- Get several containers together and some different things to put in them. Sweets taken from a variety pack are a good choice as you can eat the codes later!

- Pick two or three items that are going to be your code and share them across the containers.

- Put some of the other items into the containers to try to distract your friends.

- Give your friends one minute to crack the code. Whoever is the winner gets to set the next code.

Introducing breaking codes

3 Improve your skills

Codes with two letters will have two different elements that change.

The trick to doing these questions is to ignore the images to begin with and look at the letters underneath. Find two codes that share a letter. Then see what is the same and what is different in the images with the shared letter.

Understanding codes with two letters

Here are the most common changes that are used in questions for codes with two letters:

shape   size   shading/patterns   number   orientation   groups of shapes

Remember that you need to tackle these questions one change at a time. Work out what's happening for the first letter in the pair before looking at the second letter.

You use these sorting skills when you tidy your room. Toys go in one cupboard and clothes can either be hung up or put in a drawer. With these questions you are just working out someone else's way of sorting.

Code skills

Codes where everything in the images changes

1   The first thing to do is look for two codes with the same first letter.

   AQ   CQ   AP   BR   ?

   - AQ is a black pentagon; AP is a shaded pentagon. What does the first letter of the code tell you?

     As both shapes are pentagons, letter A must mean pentagon. So the first letter in the code tells you what the shape is.

2   Now you know what the first letter represents, you can work out what each first letter means.

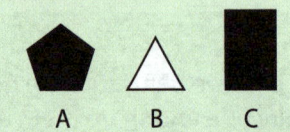

   A   B   C

   - What shapes are represented by the first letters A, B and C?

     A is a pentagon; B is a triangle; C is a rectangle. In some questions you'll only see a letter once in all four codes.

3   Now repeat the process for the second letter. Look for two codes with the same second letter.

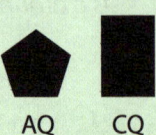

   AQ   CQ

   - AQ is a black pentagon; CQ is a black rectangle. What does the second letter of the code tell you?

     You know that the first letter tells you the shape, so the second letter must tell you the colour. In this case, Q means the shape is black.

4   Now you know what the second letter represents, you can work out what each second letter means.

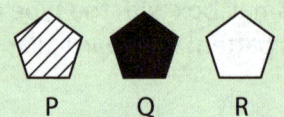

   P   Q   R

   - What colour (or patterns) do the letters P, Q and R represent?

     P is a shaded pattern; Q is; black R is white.

5   You have broken the code. Look at the shape and colour of the last image to work out the solution.

   CR

   - The shape is a white rectangle. Rectangles have the letter C; white shapes have the letter R.

     The code for the final image is CR.

Breaking codes

Codes with two letters

Codes where something in the image does not change

1. Start by looking for two codes that begin with the same first letter.

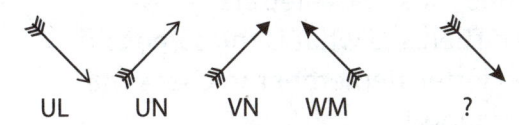

   UL   UN   VN   WM   ?

   - UL: an arrow pointing down and right; three tail fins; head with two lines.
   - UN: an arrow pointing up and right; three tail fins; head with two lines.

   That's not helpful. The first letter could mean that the arrow is pointing to the right in general, that it's got three tail fins or that the head is made up of two lines.

2. Now look for two codes with the same second letter.

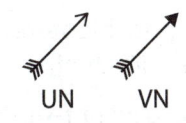

   UN   VN

   - UN: an arrow pointing up and right; three tail fins; head with two lines.
   - VN: an arrow pointing up and right; three tail fins; head is a triangle.

   Both arrows are pointing up and to the right, and both have three tail fins. But the heads are different, so the first letter must represent the style of arrow head.

3. Now you can look for differences to sort out what each first letter represents. What type of arrow head does each first letter represent?

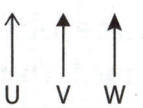

   U   V   W

   - U: an arrow head made up of two lines.
   - V: an arrow head that's a triangle.
   - W: an arrow head that's a triangle with a curved base.

4. Now decide what the second letter represents. What differences can you see?

   All the arrows have three tail fins, so this is a distraction you can ignore. But the arrows are pointing in different directions, which tells you that the second letter represents the direction of the arrow head.

5. Now you can work out what each of the second letters mean. What direction are the arrows pointing?

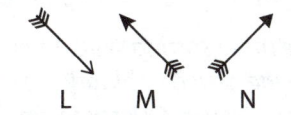

   L   M   N

   - L: an arrow pointing down and right.
   - M: an arrow pointing up and left.
   - N: an arrow pointing up and right.

6. You've broken the code. Look at the last arrow to work out the solution.

   The arrow head looks like a triangle with a curved base – W; the arrow is pointing down and to the right – L.

   WL

   The code for the final arrow is WL.

TEST YOURSELF

The four boxes on the left each have a code. Work out how the codes go with these boxes. Now find the correct code from the list on the right that matches the fifth boxes. Draw a circle round the letter under the correct code.

AM	CL	BM	CN		?		AL	CM	BN	AN	BL
							a	b	c	d	e

27

Codes with three letters

3 Improve your skills

Codes with three letters can be quite tricky so you will need to concentrate hard. You will be looking for three different elements that change.

You need to ignore the images to begin with and look at the letters underneath. Find two codes that share a letter. Then see what is the same and what is different in the images with the shared letter. Remember to check that the other two letters in the codes have both changed.

Understanding codes with three letters

Here are the most common changes that are used in questions for codes with three letters:

| shape | size | shading/patterns |
| number | orientation | groups of shapes | reflection |

Sometimes each letter in the code will have three possible states. Sometimes one of them might only have two possible states, especially if reflection is involved.

You may use these sorting skills when you are choosing what T-shirt to wear. You may decide on a combination of white or coloured, plain or patterned and short- or long-sleeved. Questions on codes are about working out what elements someone else has used to sort things.

Three-letter code skills

1 The first thing to do is look for two codes with the same first letter.

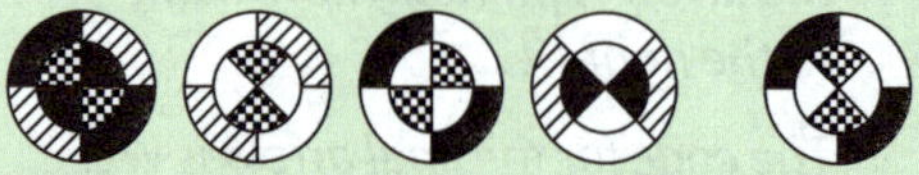

DLT   CJR   DKR   BJS   ?

- DLT has two segmented circles that line up with each other along a vertical line. The outer segments are black or striped. The inner segments are black or chequered.

- DKR has two segmented circles that line up with each other along a vertical line. The outer segments are black or white. The inner segments are white or chequered.

The only common elements are the way the circles line up with each other and the two black outer quarters.

2 Now you know what the first letter represents, you can work out what each first letter means.

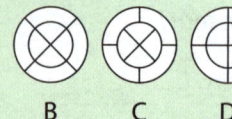

B   C   D

- B is two segmented circles that line up with each other on a diagonal line.

- C is two segmented circles that do not line up with each other.

- D is two segmented circles that line up with each other on a vertical line.

With three-letter codes it is more likely that you'll only see some letters once in the four codes.

Breaking codes

Codes with three letters

3. Now do the same for the second letter. Look for two codes with the same second letter.

   CJR   BJS

   - CJR has outer segments that are white and striped. The inner segments are white and chequered.
   - BJS has outer segments that are white and striped. The inner segments are black and white.

   The outer segments have the same pattern.

4. Now you know what the second letter represents, you can work out what each second letter means.

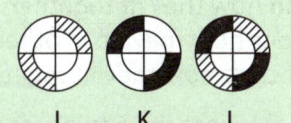

   J   K   L

   - J is a white and striped outer segment.
   - K is a black and white outer segment.
   - L is a black and striped outer segment.

   What do you think the third letter will represent?

5. Do the same for the third letter. Look for two codes with the same third letter.

   CJR   DKR

   - CJR has outer segments that are white and striped. The inner segments are white and chequered.
   - DKR has outer segments that are black and white. The inner segments are white and chequered.

   The inner segments have the same pattern.

6. Now you know what the third letter represents, you can work out what each third letter means.

   R   S   T

   - R is a white and chequered inner segment.
   - S is a black and white inner segment.
   - T is a black and chequered inner segment.

7. You have broken the code. Look at the last shape to work out the solution.

   CKR

   - The two circles do not line up – C.
   - The outer segments are shaded black and white – K.
   - The inner segments are white and chequered – R.

   The code for the final image is CKR.

TEST YOURSELF

The four shapes on the left each have a code. Work out how the codes go with these shapes. Now find the correct code from the list on the right that matches the fifth shape. Draw a circle round the letter under the correct code.

EJX   DHY   DIZ   EJY   ?   DHZ   EHX   DJY   EIX   EHZ
                                       a   b   c   d   e

29

3 Improve your skills

Finding relationships is all about spotting how images are linked together. In this section you'll see that there is often more than one connection taking place. When this happens, it is called a *relationship*.

The key to understanding these questions is to look at what is going on from one image to the next. Sometimes it can be a good idea to draw light lines to connect the elements.

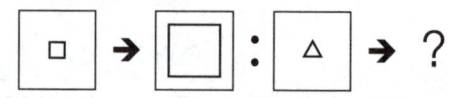

What to expect

Here are some of the changes that you will see when finding relationships:

| shape | size | shading | number of shapes |
| position | variety of shapes | | angles |

These changes will often be combined with each other or with new **connections** – such as rotation and reflection – to create a **relationship**. You could almost write a story about what is happening from one box to the next!

Some new connections can involve jigsaw-like pieces and how they fit together. In some questions they will line up so that it's fairly obvious how they fit. In other questions they'll be the wrong way round so it's not that clear how they fit together.

Irregular shapes will be used more often. These are shapes where the angles are not all the same as each other, and the sides are different lengths.

Skills in spotting the relationships
Pairs questions

1. The most common type of question in finding relationships is the 'pairs question'. You'll be shown two images that are related. You'll need to work out what has happened to get from the first image to the second one. You'll then be shown an unrelated image and asked what it would look like if the same changes were made to it.

   - Have a look at these two images and describe what has happened.

   Shading – the shapes have swapped their shading.

   Reflection – the whole image has been reflected in a horizontal mirror line.

2. Now that you know what has happened to these two images, you can work out what the boat image will look like if the same changes are made to it.

   - What 'connections' do you need to make?

   The first step is to 'swap the shading' – what was black in the first box is now white in the second box and what was white in the first box is now black in the second box.

   The next step is to 'reflect' the complete image in a horizontal mirror line. The third box shows this change. It generally doesn't matter in what order the changes take place, but try to be consistent because that way you'll remember to do each step.

Finding relationships

Relationships with more connections

1. Have a look at the two boxes.
   - How many connections go together to make up this relationship?

   The circle gets smaller.

   The circle changes from black to white.

   The trapezium gets bigger.

   The trapezium changes from white to black.

   Both shapes appear to rotate 90° anticlockwise.

   You've got five connections making up the relationship.

   - Now try to make the relationship a little more general.

   The two shapes swap their shading.

   The two shapes swap their approximate size.

   The whole box rotates 90° anticlockwise about the middle of the box.

2. In your mind, try to apply the same relationship to this image.
   - How do the connections change this image?

   The larger shape should get smaller – that's the hexagon in this example.

   The smaller shape should get bigger.

   The black shape should become white.

   The white shape should become black.

   Both shapes should rotate 90° anticlockwise.

   - Taking the changes one step at a time is always the best approach to getting the right answer.

   Even if you think the answer is obvious, take a few seconds to check that the obvious answer isn't there to catch you out.

   - Imagine you have to come up with the next box in the sequence. What would it look like?

   Now the hexagon is the larger shape and is black and the square is the smaller shape and is white.

TIPS FOR SUCCESS

Pattern spotting

Patterns are all around you. They might be in the carpet, maybe in flowers or even in the spokes of the wheels on a bike or car. Take some time to look for patterns and then imagine what would happen if you rotated or reflected them.

What you will learn

In this section you will learn these finding relationship skills:

- How to spot different relationships
- The three different types of reflection
- How there's more to rotation than a simple twist
- How to apply relationships to a shape.

31

3 Improve your skills

Changing shapes is all about the relationship between the shapes in one box and what happens to them to get to the shapes in the next box.

The trick to doing these questions is to take one element at a time and see how it changes. This can then lead on to patterns between different shapes and shading styles.

Understanding changing shapes

There are lots of things you can alter to change shapes:

> shape   size   shading
> proportion   combination of shapes

This sort of question can often have several shapes with different changes happening to each shape.

Remember that if a change is possible, the opposite change is also possible. For example, if a shape can get bigger, it can also get smaller.

Skills in spotting changes

Simple changes

Here are some of the simple changes you will see:

- The simplest change you will see is that a shape changes 'size', but stays in proportion.

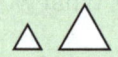

- Shapes can be 'stretched' or 'squashed'. Often one side of a shape stays the same while the other sides change.

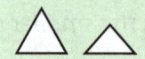

- The 'shading' of a shape can be changed. The shading can be solid black, solid white or a pattern.

Simple changes can also be combined. For example, the shape might become bigger but also get a different shading pattern.

TRY IT OUT

Word play

Here's a quick way to play with shapes – use Microsoft® Word on your computer.

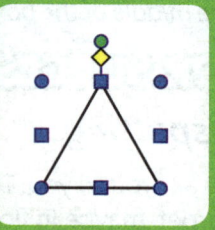

- Place a shape on the screen.
- Select the shape so that the boxes and circles appear around it.
- Click and hold on one of the circles in the corner and hold the 'Shift' key down (as you would to make a capital letter).
- Move the mouse. The shape will get smaller and bigger in proportion.
- Release the 'Shift' key and you can adjust the proportion as well.

Finding relationships

Changing shapes

Linked changes

1 In some questions the changes to the shapes are 'linked'.

- Have a look at these two boxes. They both contain squares, triangles and circles, but there are different numbers of each and they are all in different positions. What are the similarities?

The two identical shapes are on the top row.

There are four shapes in each box.

If you look more closely you can see that where the squares were, you now have triangles. Where the triangle was you now have a circle and where the circle was you now have a square. The shapes have all changed in order.

2 In some questions the shapes are the same, but you can see that the shading has changed.

- What changes are shown in these two boxes?

The shape that was black is now white.

The shapes that were white are now striped.

The shape that was striped is now black.

This example has three different shading patterns, but you can sometimes have four.

TIPS FOR SUCCESS

Three's company

Many of these changes happen in threes, so take some time to work with changing things in sequences of threes. It could be anything, even a knife, fork and spoon if you are waiting for something to cook.

TEST YOURSELF

The two boxes on the left are a pair. Work out which of the five boxes on the right completes the second pair in the same way as the first pair. Circle the letter under the box that you think is the correct answer.

1

2

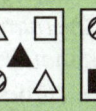

33

3 Improve your skills

Number and proportion questions are a little surprising as there are no numbers in them. Think of them more as being about quantity rather than number.

In number questions you will be looking at how many corners or shapes there are. For proportion, you might look at how much of a shape is shaded overall.

Understanding number and proportion

Number questions can be some of the most confusing questions as a pattern is not always obvious. You'll look at pictures of different shapes and wonder what the link is. Often number is the last thing you'll try once you have discounted all the other options.

Proportion questions are often easier than number questions and involve segmented shapes. To answer these questions you'll might need to look at…

  rotation   reflection   shading

The skill that is used in most proportion questions is shading.

Square paper can be a useful tool for getting used to what different proportions look like. You can draw boxes and shade in different numbers of squares. Some squares might not be touching.

Skills in number questions

A constant number

In these questions, something about the shapes in the boxes has a constant number.

- At first glance these two boxes seem to have nothing in common. What is it about the shapes in these two boxes that has a constant number?

The first box has two rectangles and two triangles. The second box has two pentagons and a rectangle.

The shading of all the shapes is the same but the number of shapes is different. Even though both boxes have at least one rectangle, the rectangles are not the same size or in the same position.

Knowing that the number of shapes is different means you can rule out rotation and reflection without going any further.

If you count the number of corners the shapes have, you will find that there are 14 corners in both boxes.

Now you need to check each of the possible answers to see which of them also has 14 corners. Do check them all, even if the first seems to fit. If there's more than one with the right number of corners, you might find that something else is also important. It might be that the shapes are all white, or maybe there always has to be one specific shape, such as the rectangle in this example.

Finding relationships

A changing number

In some questions you'll see numbers that increase or decrease in regular steps. These questions are covered in more detail in number patterns on pages 62–65.

- These boxes contain a series of shapes. No two boxes are the same and none of the shapes inside the boxes match each other. In this sort of question you are often asked what comes next in the pattern.

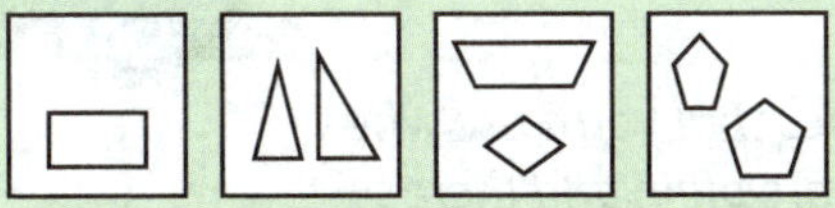

The first box has a rectangle; the second has two triangles; the third has a trapezium and a diamond; the last has two pentagons.

If you look at the number of corners, you can see that the first box has four, the second has six, the third has eight, and the last has ten.

The pattern is that the number of corners is going up by two each time. That means the next box will have 12 corners. The shapes could be two hexagons, or three quadrilaterals or even four triangles, but there will be 12 corners.

Skills in proportion questions

Segments and shading

Proportion questions will generally involve a number of identical shapes or large shapes broken up into a number of segments.

- Have a look at these two shapes. What proportion has been shaded in each one?

In the first shape every other segment is shaded, so you can say half of the shape is shaded.

In the second shape pairs of segments are shaded, but it's still half the shape that is shaded.

In both shapes half of the segments are shaded black. Imagine you have to draw the shape that will match these two shapes. What will it look like?

Will all the shaded segments be together?

Will you put the shaded segments in pairs, individually or mix them up?

As long as four out of the eight segments are shaded, the answer will be correct.

Number and proportion

TEST YOURSELF

There are two similar boxes on the left. Work out which of the five boxes on the right is most like the first two. Circle the letter under the box that you think is the correct answer.

1

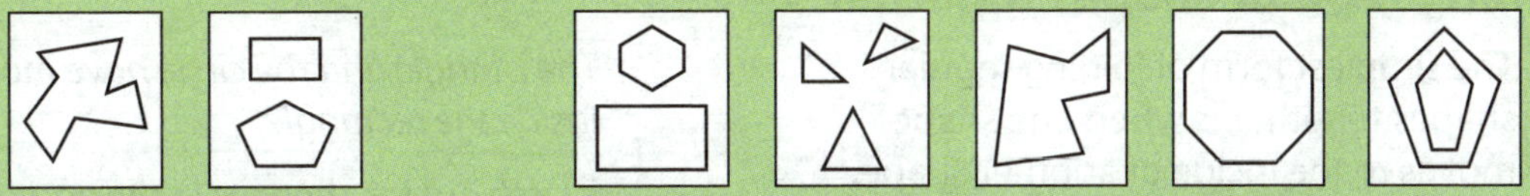

                              a   b   c   d   e

2

                              a   b   c   d   e

3 Improve your skills

Moving and connecting shapes is all about rearranging shapes and putting them together or taking them apart.

These questions can involve irregular shapes that look like jigsaw pieces or moving one shape inside another. Sometimes you'll see that one element from the image will move but the rest will remain the same.

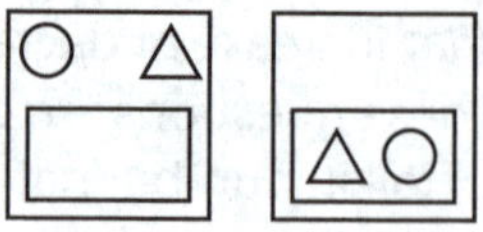

Understanding moving and connecting shapes

As the shapes move around the box they will sometimes be **rotated** but not reflected.

Many of the skills in connecting shapes are the same ones that you'd use when doing a jigsaw puzzle. The difference is that the shapes are plain and there's no picture to help you – it's a bit like doing the puzzle with all the pieces turned over.

Skills in moving shapes

Moving apart

1. The simplest form of moving apart is when one shape moves from inside another shape to outside it.
   - Can you see what is happening to the shapes in these two boxes on the right?

   Usually the shapes that move will stay the same size and the same way up, as in this example.

2. Sometimes a shape leaves a hole behind when it moves.
   - The square in this box has moved from inside the circle to outside.

   The size of the shapes is the same. The shading is different. 

   Depending on how you think, you'll either call it a hole or say another square has been added. As long as you can spot the connection, it doesn't matter how you think about it.

Joining regular shapes together

1. The simplest form of joining regular shapes together is when one shape moves to the inside of another shape. Generally when this happens you'll see one shape that is bigger than the others and the smaller shapes move inside it.
   - How have the regular shapes in the two boxes on the right joined?

The triangle and the circle have moved inside the rectangle.

Watch out for changes in the positions of the shapes, as in this example – if the shapes swap sides, it will be important to the answer.

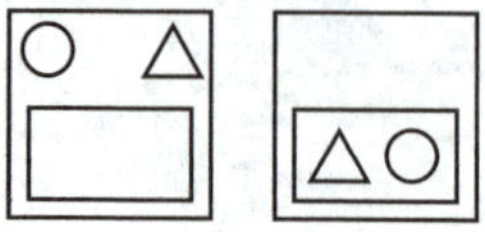

36

Finding relationships

2 In some questions, when shapes join together they seem to make an extra shape.

- Here are four triangles joined together at the corners so it looks like you've added a square. If you take away each triangle in turn, the lines that make the square will disappear as well.

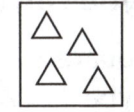

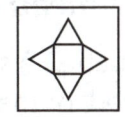

  Look closely at the triangles that seem to have a square in the middle. Does the image remind you of anything? It's the net of a square-based pyramid.

3 Some shapes, especially identical shapes, can join together along their sides to make a pattern that fits closely together (tessellates).

- How have these triangles been joined?

  Occasionally shapes that are not identical can be joined together like this.

Joining irregular shapes together

Irregular shapes will often look like jigsaw pieces with bits that stick out of one piece and fit into another.

- Will these two irregular shapes join together?

  Like most jigsaw pieces, these shapes will join up to make a more recognisable shape – a rectangle in this example.

  You will not always be shown the shapes so that they line up. You may have to rotate them before you can join them together.

  The questions may try to trip you up by swapping the shading when the pieces are joined together or by turning the pieces upside down. Remember that many questions will use more than one relationship.

TRY IT OUT

Pattern pieces

Next time you have a wet break time in school, see if you can use the construction kits to make some tessellating patterns with triangles or squares.

- Use no more than five pieces at a time.
- Draw the patterns you create so that you can look at them as you prepare for the test.

TEST YOURSELF

The two boxes on the left are a pair. Work out which of the five boxes on the right completes the second pair in the same way as the first pair. Circle the letter under the box that you think is the correct answer.

Moving and connecting shapes

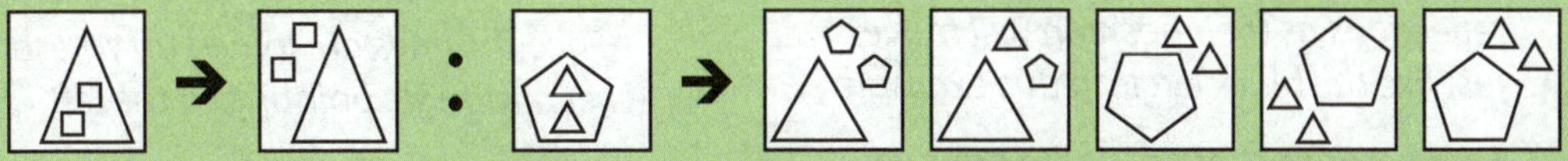

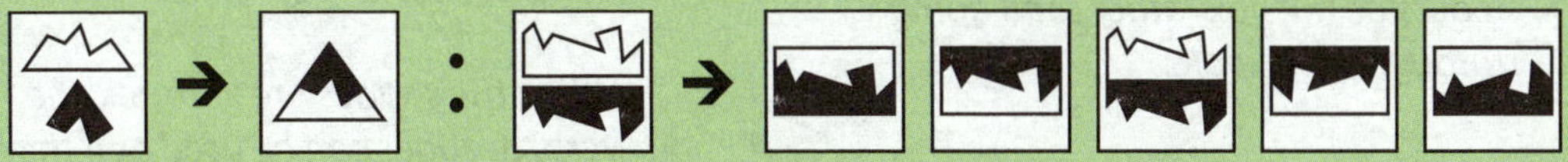

3 Improve your skills

Reflections in vertical lines

Reflections are another type of relationship that you will see and most question types can use reflections. Although you won't be shown a dotted mirror line that doesn't mean you can't draw one in.

Sometimes the **reflection** is inside a shape such as a square. Perhaps the **shading patterns** will be reflected, or maybe the shapes inside.

Understanding reflections in vertical lines

Reflections in vertical lines are the most common type of reflections as they are slightly easier to understand when the images are in a row.

As you start to get used to these types of questions, try working with a ruler. Remember that each point on each shape will end up the same distance from the mirror line, but on the opposite side of the line, so you can use the ruler to check what you do.

Reflections in vertical lines can be seen as reflections in a big mirror, such as those you see on wardrobe doors. If you have a mirror like this at home, sit beside it and hold up various shapes to find out how they are reflected.

Reflection skills

Positioning the mirror line

Remember that a box can often contain several shapes. Sometimes just one shape is reflected, but usually you are looking at a reflection of the complete box.

- Look at the mirror line for the box reflected here.

  Shapes that are not in the middle of the box can give you big clues about reflections as their position will move, just like the black circle in this example.

  For questions that are not in grids you need to imagine that your mirror line is outside the box rather than going through the middle.

Reflections in a vertical line

1 The simplest reflection is that of a single shape.

- Look at this triangle, which is pointing to the right.

  Imagine that there is a mirror line just beyond the point on the right-hand side.

  Each point has to travel to that imaginary line and then the same distance past it.

  Once the lines are joined up you should get a triangle pointing to the left.

  When the shapes are in boxes, the vertical edges can be used as if they are mirror lines.

38

Finding relationships

Reflections in vertical lines

2. The second type of reflection in a vertical line involves shading.

- This overall shape is an equilateral triangle that is pointing up. If it didn't have any shading the reflection would be the same as the original shape.

  Once again, imagine a mirror line just to the right of the triangle.

  Each point has to travel to that line and the same distance past it, and that includes the point on the base where the edge of the shading is.

  Working out where the shading patterns are can be tricky. Put a point in the middle of each area and treat it like the other points.

  You should come up with a shape where the shading seems to have swapped over.

3. The final type of reflection in a vertical line involves more than one shape.

- Here you have an equilateral triangle with a square and a circle inside it.

  Put that imaginary mirror line in on the right-hand side again and reflect the triangle.

  You can reflect the square in the same way – you've got four corners to work with.

  You should find that the circle and the square seem to swap places inside the triangle.

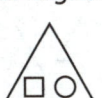

TRY IT OUT

Look up, look down, look around

Reflections can be seen all around us, sometimes without a mirror, pond or any sort of reflective surface.

Have a look at how many reflections you can see around you and how many are not quite reflections:

- car wheels (Is the rear wheel a reflection of the front wheel? Ignore the logo in the middle for this question.)
- bricks in a wall
- the shapes of shop windows
- paving slabs
- tiles on the floor and the walls.

How many reflections can you find in 15 minutes?

TEST YOURSELF

The first two images on the left are a pair. Work out which of the five images on the right completes the second pair in the same way as the first pair. Circle the letter under the image that you think is the correct answer.

1.

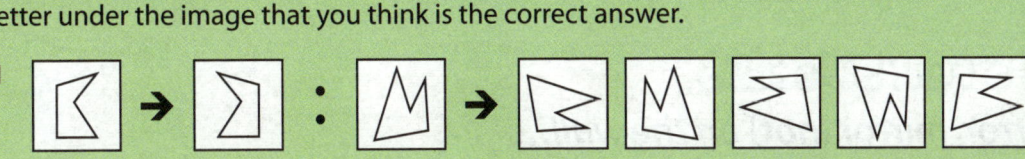

2.

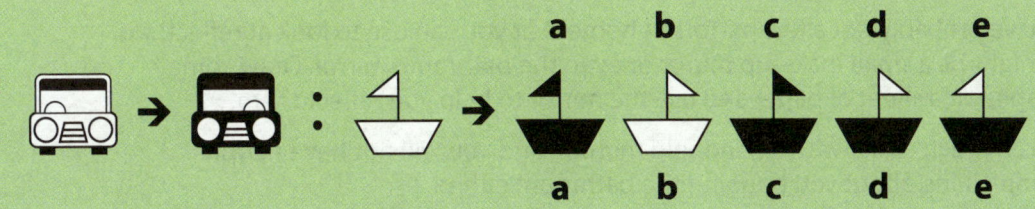

39

3 Improve your skills

Understanding reflections in other lines

There are two other types of reflection that you will generally see in questions:

reflection in a horizontal line   **reflection in a diagonal line**

Reflections in a diagonal line are not that common, but are seen every now and then. Diagonal lines in these examples are lines at 45° to the base of the box.

You can look at a reflection in a diagonal line as being a reflection in a vertical or horizontal line followed by a 90° rotation, or a 90° rotation followed by a reflection.

More reflection skills

Reflections in horizontal lines

With the exception of questions in grids, reflections in horizontal lines can be tricky to spot as the images are lined up across the page rather than down it.

- Look at this triangle. Imagine that there is a mirror line just below the shape. Remember that, generally, everything inside the box will be reflected together.

  Each point has to travel to that imaginary line and then the same distance past it.

  Once the lines are joined up in this example, you get a triangle pointing down.

  When the shapes are in boxes, the vertical edges can be used as if they are mirror lines.

  Reflections involving shading or more than one shape work in exactly the same way – only the direction has changed.

Reflections in diagonal lines

Most reflection questions use horizontal or vertical reflection lines. However, you may occasionally see a question with a diagonal reflection line at 45° to the base of the box (either inside it or outside it).

- Imagine that there is a mirror line going diagonally through this box. Use a real mirror if this helps. You will need to turn it round to check the other side of the reflection.

  Each point has to travel the shortest distance possible to that imaginary line and then the same distance past it.

  The shapes will always remain the same, but their positions will change.

  If you find it easier to think about a rotation and a reflection being combined, then use that to help you work out the answer.

TIPS FOR SUCCESS

Mirror, mirror (not) on the wall…

You've probably got a few mirrors at home that you can use to look at reflections. It might be a small make-up mirror or even the bathroom mirror. Draw some shapes on a sheet of paper and use the mirror to help you reflect them.

This is much easier with a handheld mirror – and you will not have people complaining about you hogging the bathroom either!

Finding relationships

Reflections in diagonal lines as a rotation and simpler reflection

Lots of people find that reflections in a diagonal lines are confusing as the shape seems to have to fold over itself.

You can also break this skill down into two steps to make it easier.

Start with the same shape as on page 40 and reflect it in a line that goes from top left to bottom right.

- The first step is to rotate in the direction of the lowest point on the mirror line, as that's the bottom right you need to rotate 90° clockwise.
- The final step is to reflect the rotated shape in a vertical mirror line.

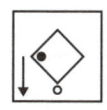

As you can see, the final answer is still the same.

- If the diagonal mirror line had been going from bottom left to top right, you would need to rotate the shape 90° anticlockwise before reflecting it in a vertical mirror line.

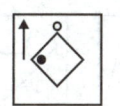

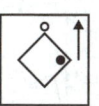

TRY IT OUT
True or false?
Play this game with a friend.

- Both of you need to fold a piece of A4 paper into quarters.
- In each quarter draw a shape and a possible reflection. Some should be true reflections and some should be wrong.
- Without using a mirror, see if you can work out which of your friend's drawings are true reflections.
- You get a point if you are correct and your friend gets a point if you are wrong.
- Your friend should do the same with your drawings.

How quickly can you get to 10 points?

TEST YOURSELF

The first two boxes on the left are a pair. Work out which of the five boxes on the right completes the second pair in the same way as the first pair. Circle the letter under the box that you think is the correct answer.

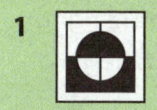

1.   a   b   c   d   e

2.   a   b   c   d   e

Reflections in horizontal and diagonal lines

41

3 Improve your skills

Rotations

Rotations are a relationship that you'll see a lot. In some questions the shapes rotate and in others the shaded segments rotate.

Rotations can be **clockwise** or **anticlockwise**. Sometimes you'll see rotations in both directions in the same question, especially where similar shapes are used one inside the other.

Understanding rotations

Rotations take place in **multiples of 45°**, so you can see rotations of…

45°	90°	135°	180°
225°	270°	315°	

Remember that a clockwise rotation of 270° is the same as an anticlockwise rotation of 90°.

This is a similar idea to looking at a clock face; 45 minutes past the hour is the same as 15 minutes to the hour.

Rotation skills

Rotation of a shape

1 The simplest rotation is that of a single shape. Have a look at these two triangles.

- You can tell that the second triangle is a rotation of the first. It's difficult to be sure how much it has been rotated as all the corners are the same.

  There will usually be more clues, possibly another shape around the triangle, or in one of the corners. There will also be more clues if you've got four images to work with rather than two.

2 This pair of shapes is 'irregular', which makes it far easier to see what happens when they are rotated.

- Use the centre of the box the shape is in. Pick two points on the shape and rotate them in your mind to see if you can match them to the second shape.
- Once you've matched the two points, use a third to check that you're right.

  In this example the shape has been rotated 45° clockwise.

  Remember that you can always rotate the paper on your table if it helps.

Making connections

Look at the five images in each row. Work out what connects *four* of the images and makes the other image the odd one out. Circle the letter under the image most *unlike* the others.

Example

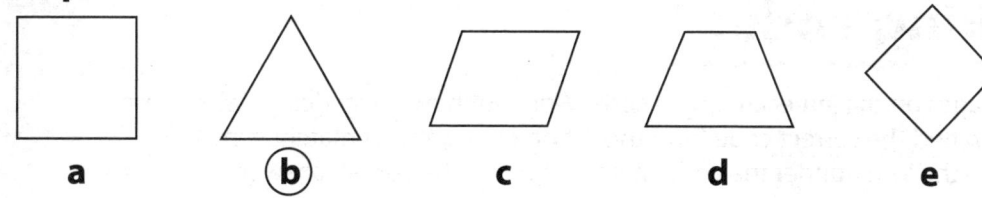

a   (b)   c   d   e

*Shapes a, c, d and e all have four sides; shape b has three sides. The shape most unlike the others is **b**.*

Now have a go at these similar questions. Circle the letter under the image that you think is most unlike the others.

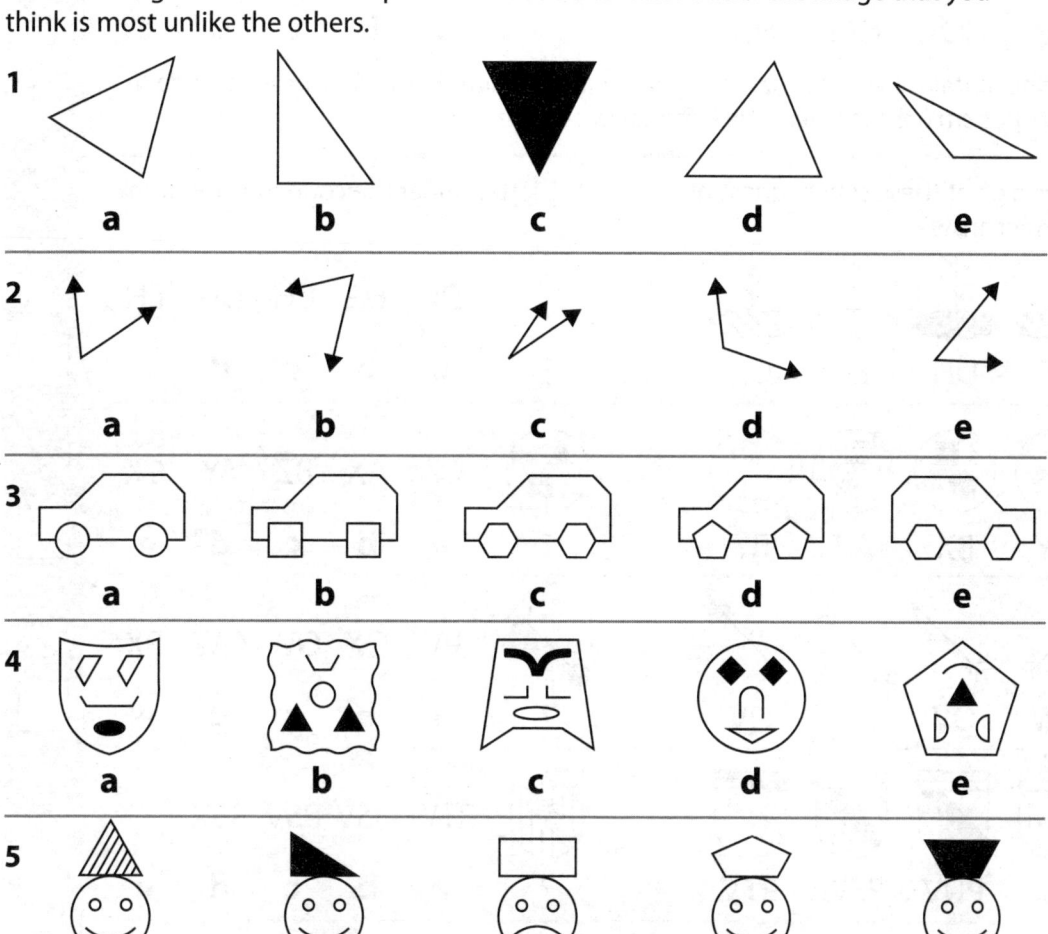

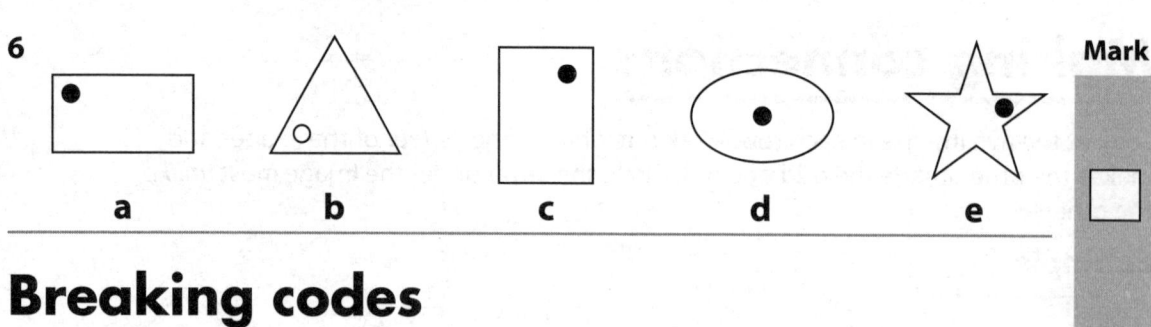

Breaking codes

The four images on the left each have a code. Work out how the codes go with these images. Now find the correct code from the list on the right that matches the fifth image. Circle the letter under the code that you think is the correct answer.

Example

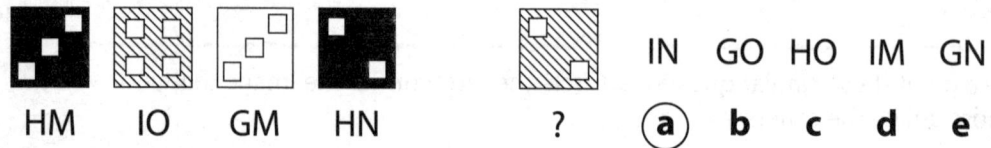

The fifth box contains two small squares and a diagonal pattern. Two has the letter code N. A diagonal pattern has the letter code I. The correct answer is **a**.

Now have a go at these similar questions. Circle the letter under the code that you think is the correct answer.

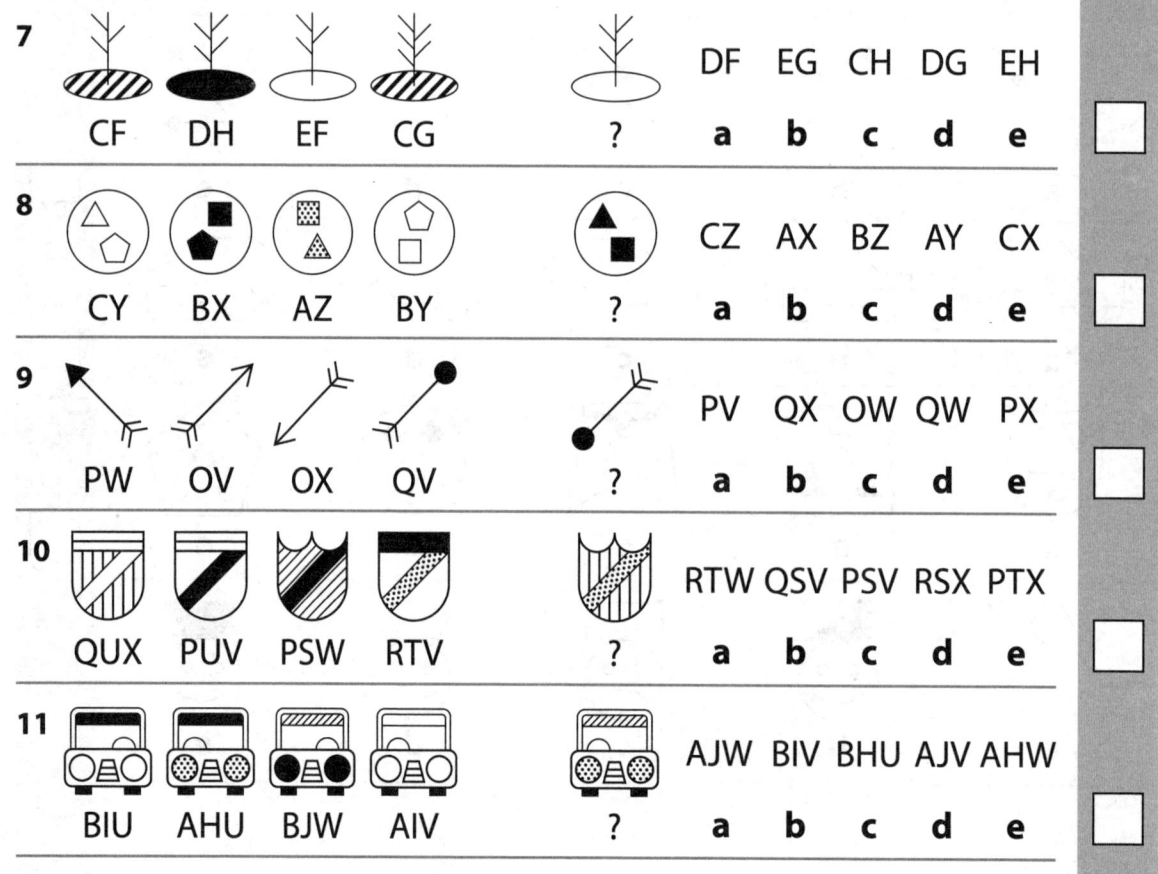

Finding relationships

Look at the pair of images on the left, connected by an arrow. Work out how the two images go together. Now look at the third image, which is followed by another arrow. Work out which of the five images on the right completes the second pair in the same way as the first pair. Circle the letter under the image that you think is the correct answer.

Example

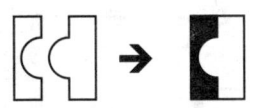

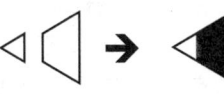

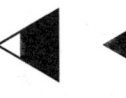

*Image 2 is formed by joining the two shapes in image 1 together, and shading the first shape black. The correct answer is **d**.*

Now have a go at these similar questions. Circle the letter under the image that you think is the correct answer.

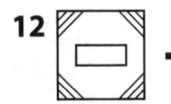

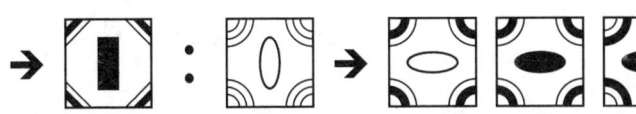

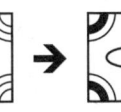

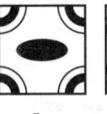

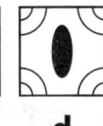

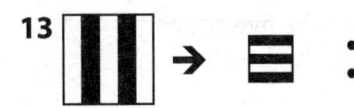

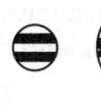

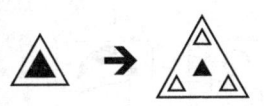

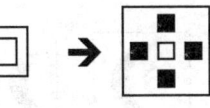

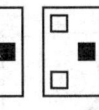

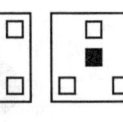

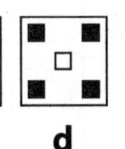

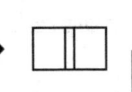

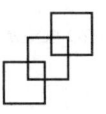

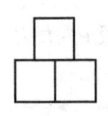

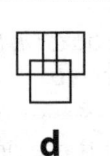

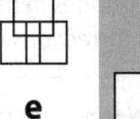

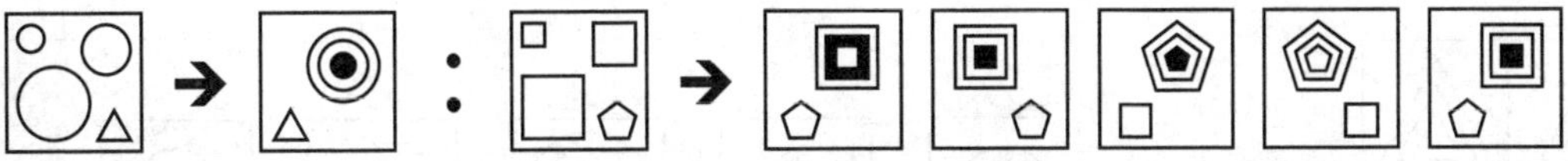

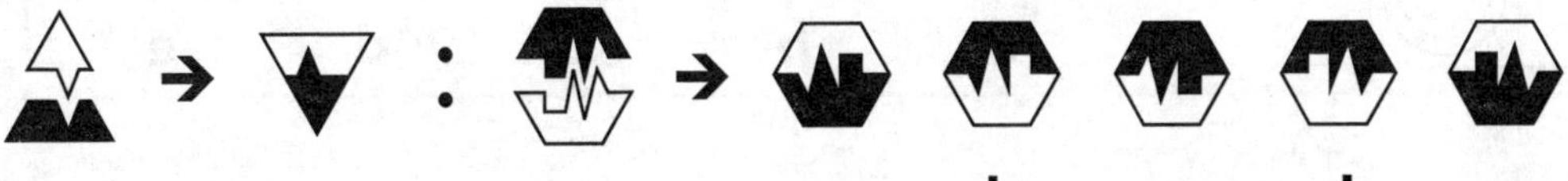

11+ Non-Verbal Reasoning Success

Practice test 1

18. ... a b c d e

19. ... a b c d e

20. ... a b c d e

21. ... a b c d e

Mark

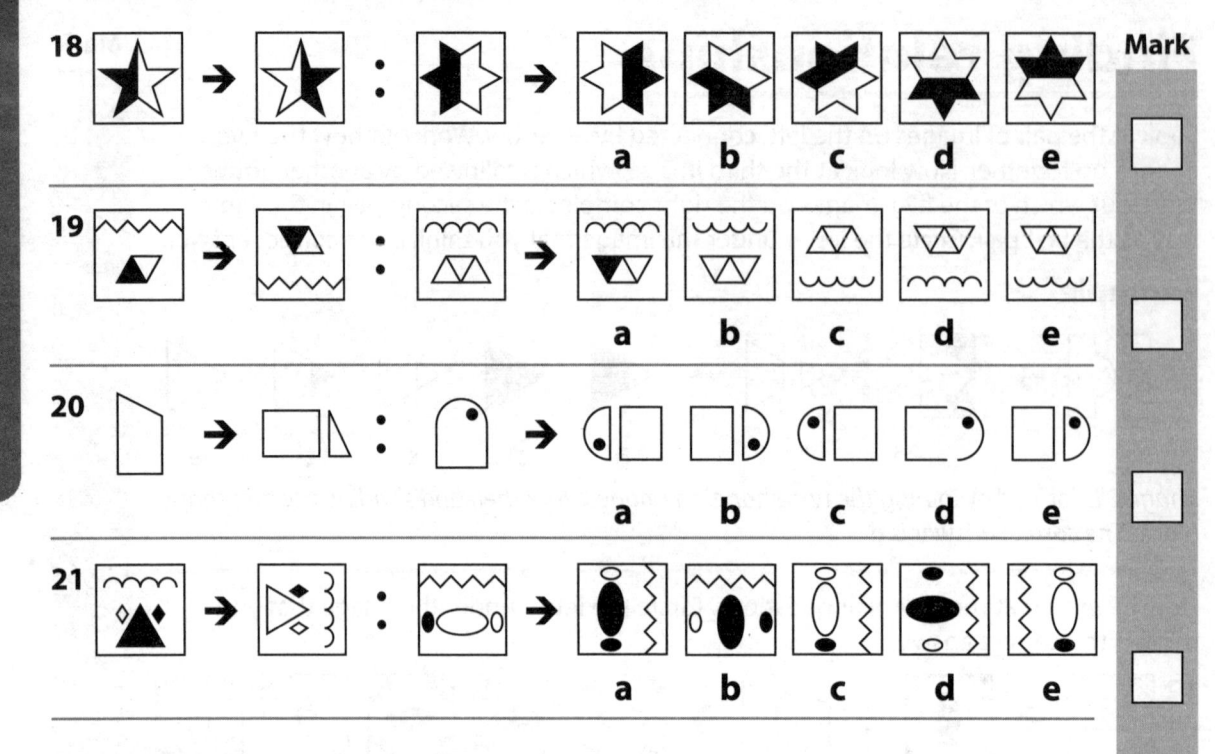

Spotting patterns

One of the boxes is missing from the grid on the left. Work out which of the five boxes on the right completes the grid. Circle the letter under the box that you think is the correct answer.

Example

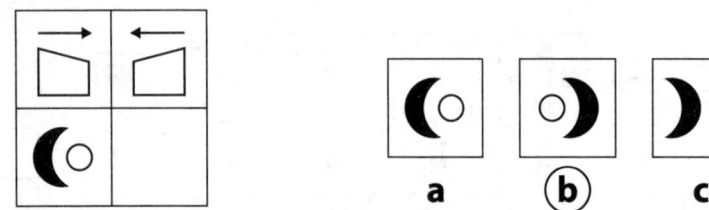

a (b) c d e

*The images in the boxes in the left-hand column are reflected vertically. The correct answer is **b**.*

Now have a go at these similar questions. Circle the letter under the box that you think is the correct answer.

22. a b c d e

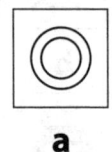

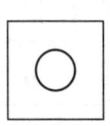

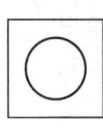

4

© Letts Educational Ltd, *an imprint of HarperCollins Publishers*

11+ Non-Verbal Reasoning Success

Mark

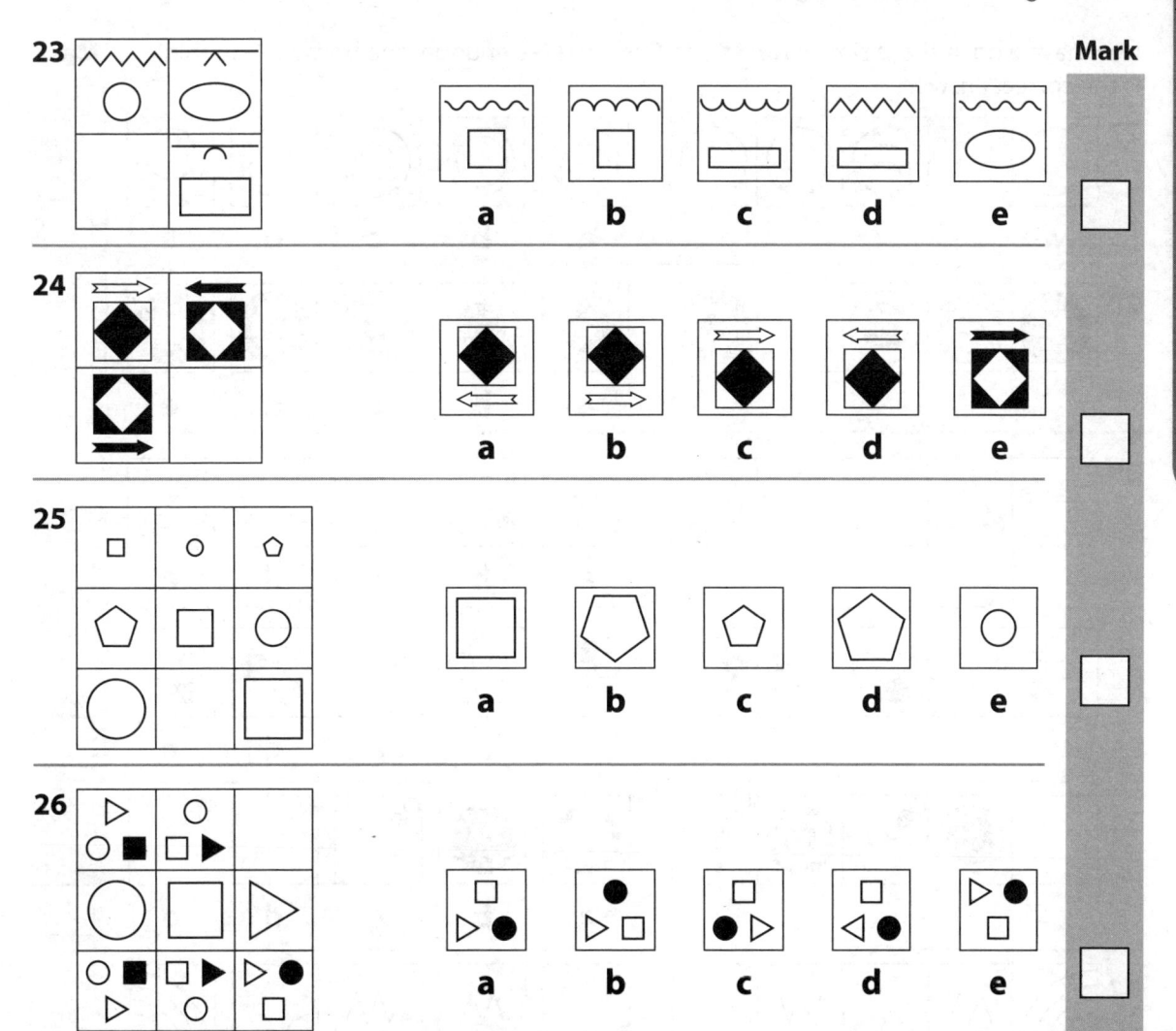

23

24

25

26

Completing sequences

One of the boxes on the right completes the sequence or pattern on the left. Circle the letter under the box that you think is the correct answer.

Example

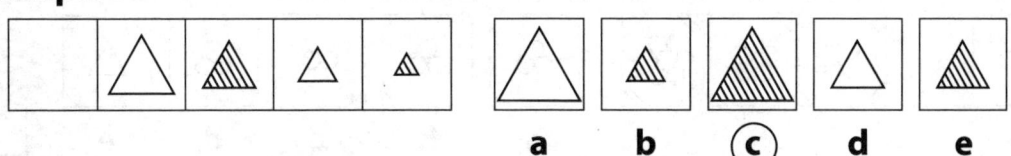

Looking from left to right, the triangle in each box decreases in size and alternates between being striped and white. The correct answer is **c**.

© Letts Educational Ltd, *an imprint of HarperCollins Publishers*

5

11+ Non-Verbal Reasoning Success

Practice test 1

Now have a go at these similar questions. Circle the letter under the box that you think is the correct answer.

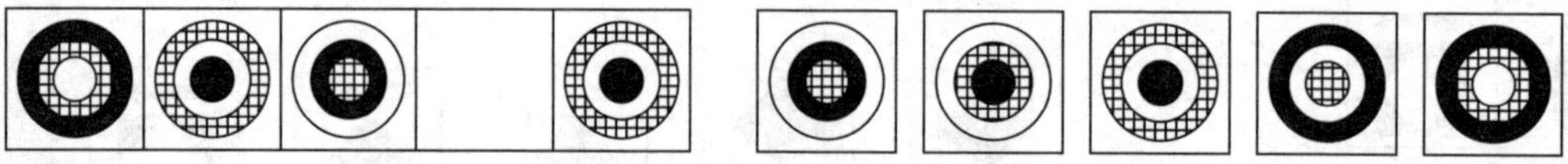

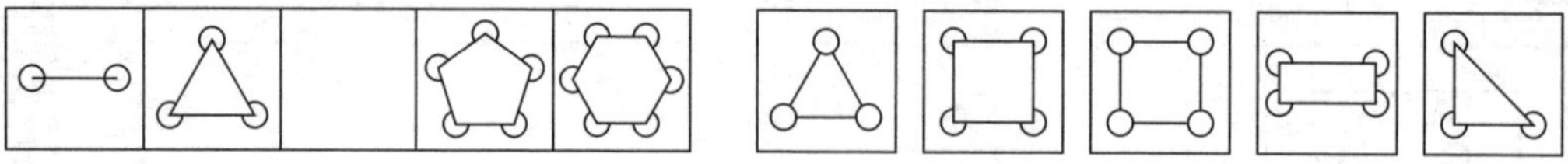

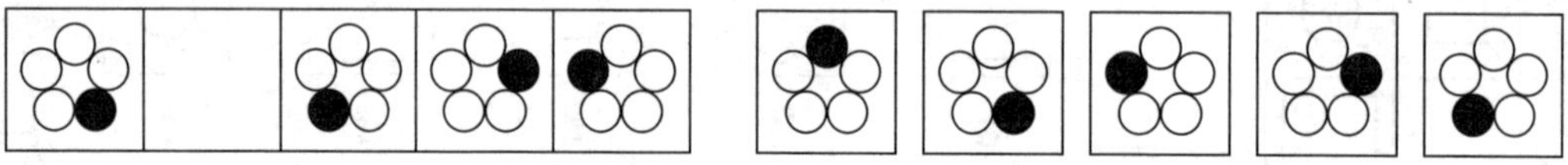

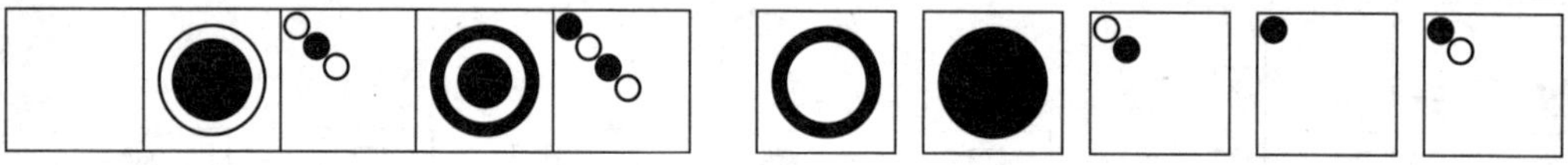

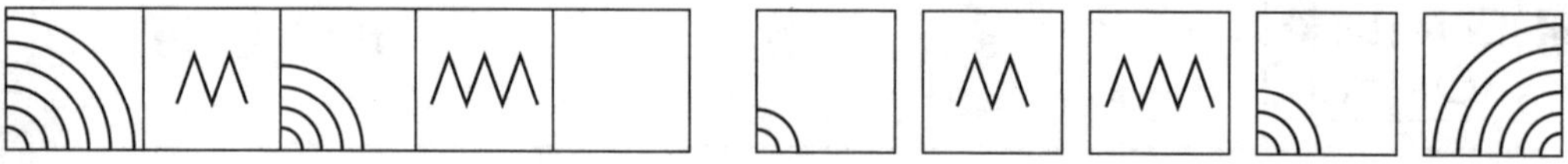

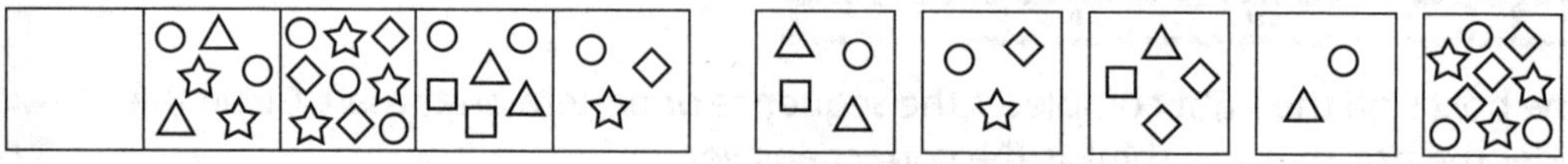

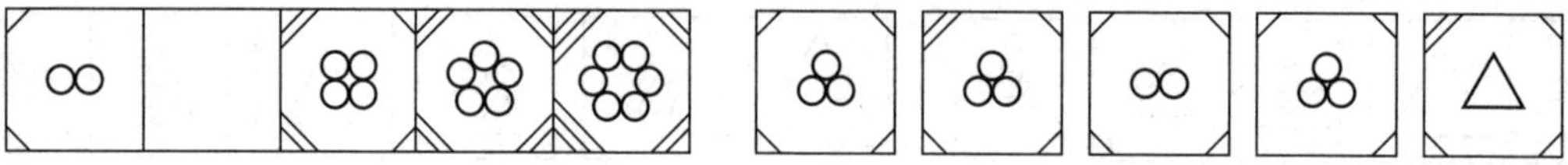

Mark

27

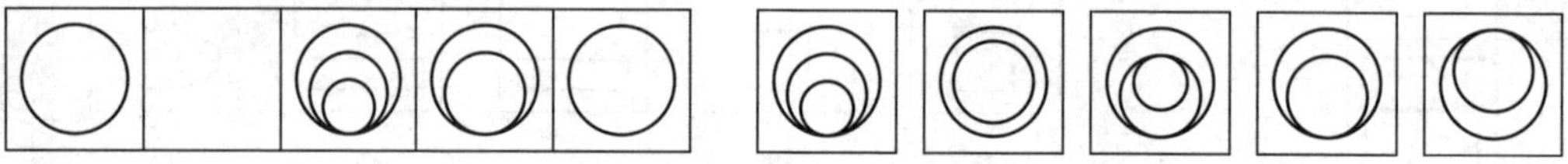

28

29

30

31

32

33

34

TEST ENDS

Making connections

Look at the two images on the left. Decide what makes these two images similar to each other. Now find the image on the right that is *most like* the two images on the left. Circle the letter under the image that you think is the correct answer.

Example

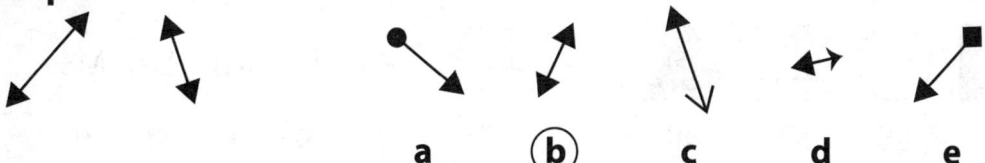

*The two images on the left have identical arrow heads at both ends of the line. Only **b** has the same arrow head at both ends.*

Now have a go at these similar questions. Circle the letter under the image that you think is *most like* the two images on the left.

Breaking codes

The four images on the left each have a code. Work out how the codes go with these images. Now find the correct code from the list on the right that matches the fifth image. Circle the letter under the code that you think is the correct answer.

Example

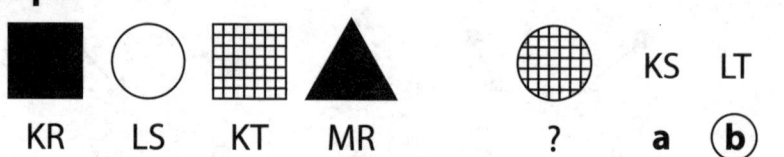

						KS	LT	MT	LR	MS
KR	LS	KT	MR	?		a	(b)	c	d	e

The fifth shape is a circle and has a hatched pattern. A circle has the letter code L. A hatched pattern has the letter code T. The answer is b.

Now have a go at these similar questions. Circle the letter under the code that you think is the correct answer.

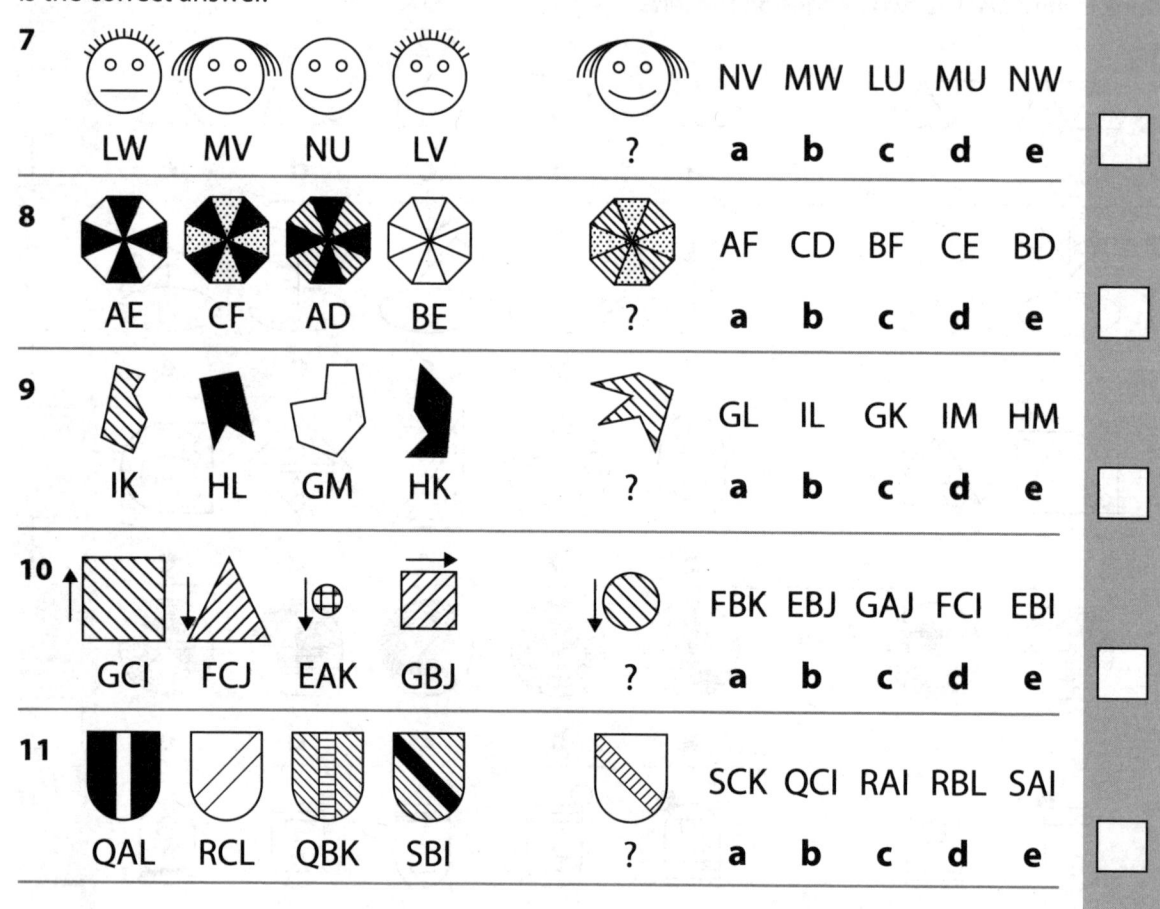

7

						NV	MW	LU	MU	NW
LW	MV	NU	LV	?		a	b	c	d	e

8

						AF	CD	BF	CE	BD
AE	CF	AD	BE	?		a	b	c	d	e

9

						GL	IL	GK	IM	HM
IK	HL	GM	HK	?		a	b	c	d	e

10

						FBK	EBJ	GAJ	FCI	EBI
GCI	FCJ	EAK	GBJ	?		a	b	c	d	e

11

						SCK	QCI	RAI	RBL	SAI
QAL	RCL	QBK	SBI	?		a	b	c	d	e

Finding relationships

Look at the pair of images on the left, connected by an arrow. Work out how the two images go together. Now look at the third image, which is followed by another arrow. Work out which of the five images on the right completes the second pair in the same way as the first pair. Circle the letter under the image that you think is the correct answer.

Example

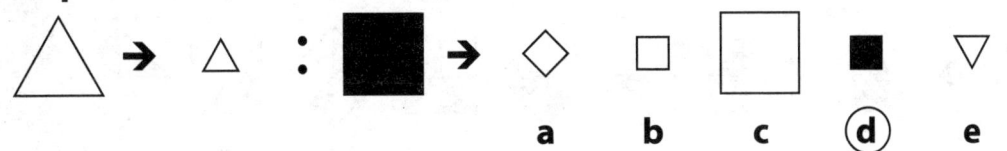

The second shape in each pair remains the same colour and is reduced in size. The answer is d.

Now have a go at these similar questions. Circle the letter under the image that you think is the correct answer.

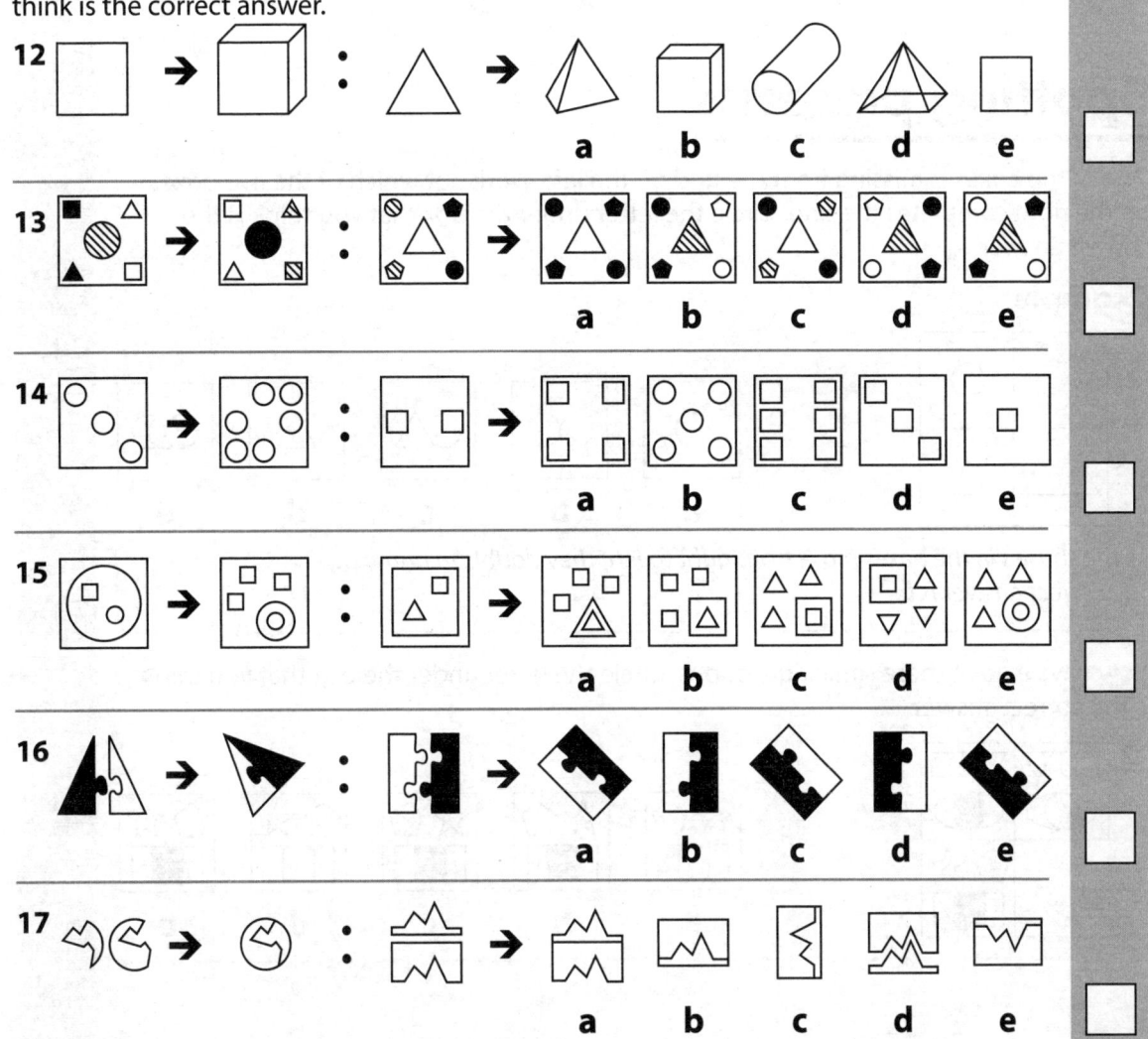

12.

13.

14.

15.

16.

17.

11+ Non-Verbal Reasoning Success

Practice test 2

18. [figure] a b c d e

19. [figure] a b c d e

20. [figure] a b c d e

21. [figure] a b c d e

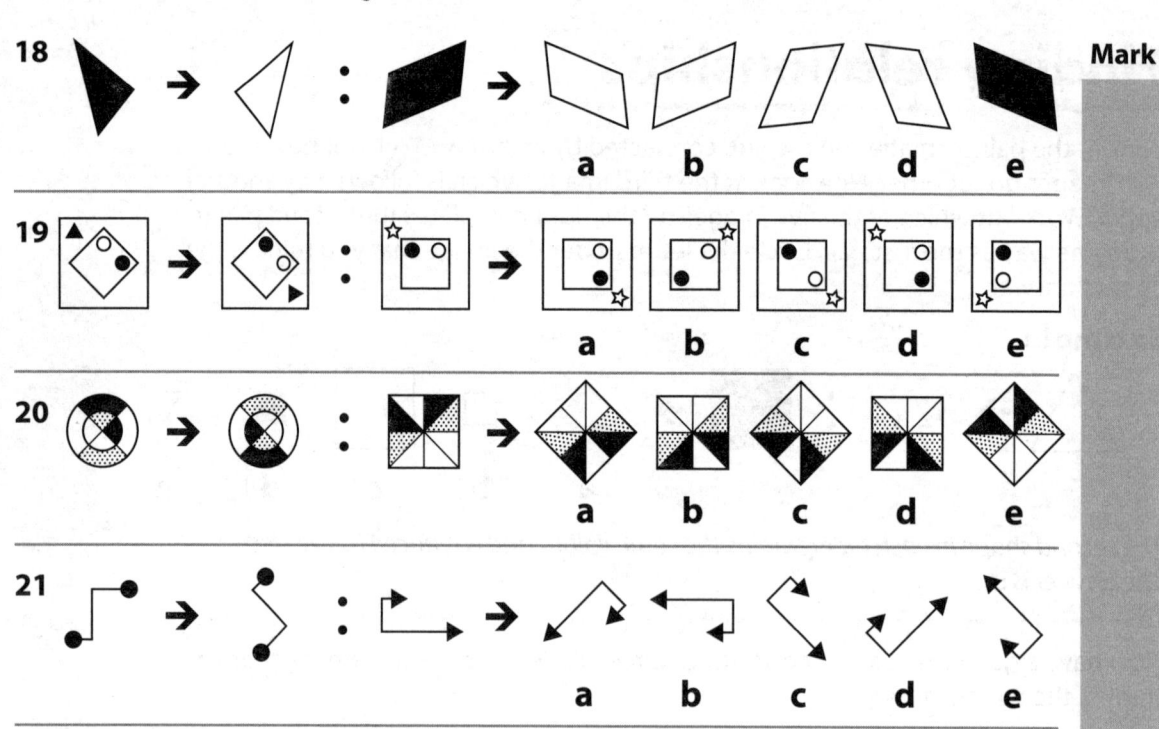

Spotting patterns

One of the boxes is missing from the grid on the left. Work out which of the five boxes on the right completes the grid. Circle the letter under the box that you think is the correct answer.

Example

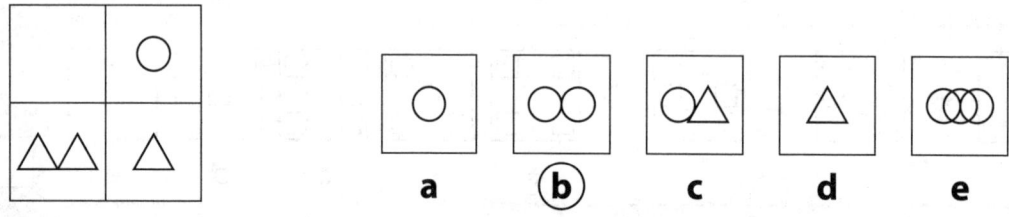

[figure] a (b) c d e

As the shapes in the boxes move from right to left, they double in number. The correct answer is **b**.

Now have a go at these similar questions. Circle the letter under the box that you think is the correct answer.

22. [figure] a b c d e

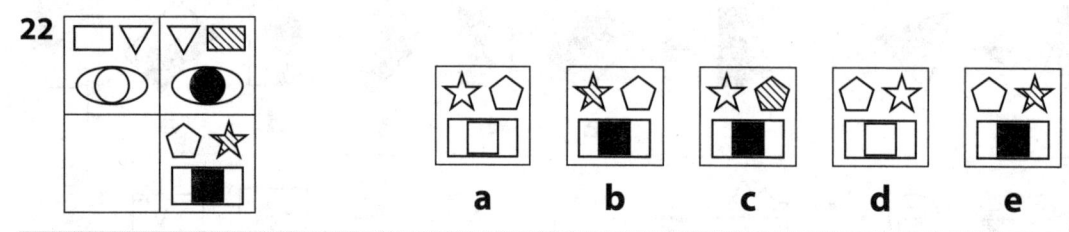

© Letts Educational Ltd, an imprint of HarperCollins Publishers

11+ Non-Verbal Reasoning Success

Practice test 2

Mark

23

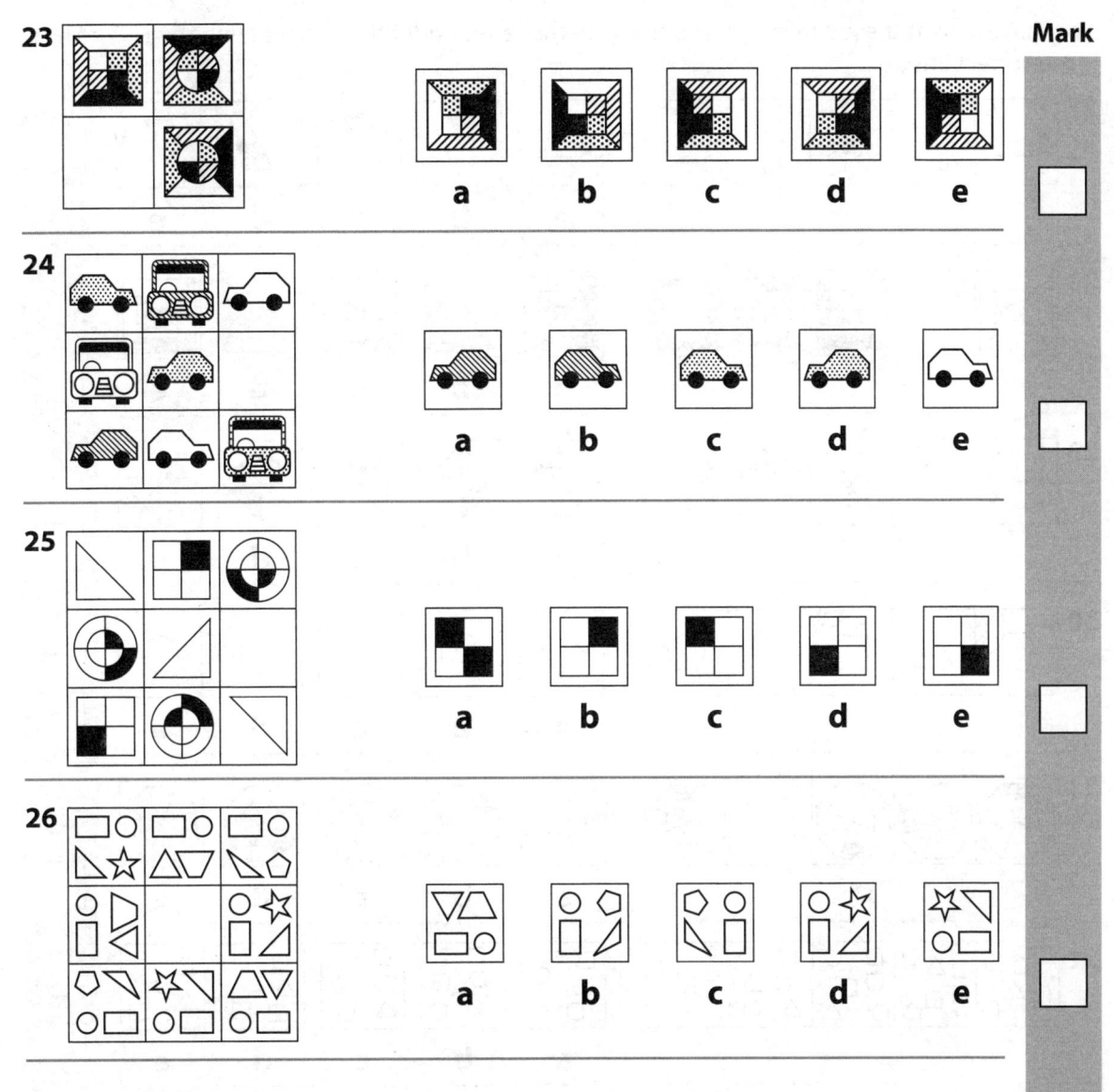

24

25

26

Completing sequences

One of the five boxes on the right completes the sequence or pattern on the left. Circle the letter under the box that you think is the correct answer.

Example

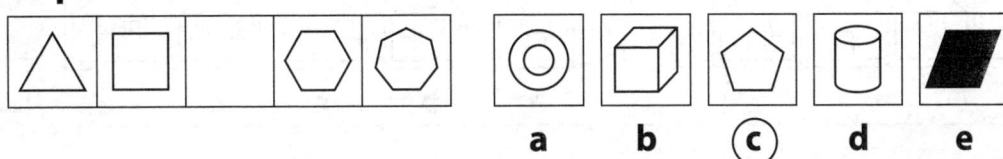

a b (c) d e

*Looking at the boxes from left to right, the number of sides on the shape increases by one each time. The correct answer is **c**.*

© Letts Educational Ltd, *an imprint of HarperCollins Publishers*

11+ Non-Verbal Reasoning Success

Now have a go at these similar questions. Circle the letter under the box that you think is the correct answer.

Mark

27 – **28** – **29** – **30** – **31** – **32** – **33** – **34**

Each question shows a sequence of figures followed by five options labelled **a**, **b**, **c**, **d**, **e**.

TEST ENDS

Finding relationships

Rotation of shaded segments

1. In this sort of question the overall shape doesn't seem to move because it's a regular shape.

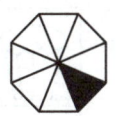

- The first step to spotting that the shaded segments have rotated is that you have the same number of each type of shading and you can find the same order going in the same direction.
- Match a segment in both shapes. In these two you can see there's just one shaded segment so they are easy to match.

   You should see that the rotation is 135° clockwise.

2. Sometimes you'll get more than one type of shading.

- Have you got the same number of segments of each type in both images? Are they in the same order?
- Match a segment in both shapes – try the white segment between the two spotted ones as it's easy to track.

   The segments have rotated 90° anticlockwise.

Two different rotation patterns

In some questions there are two different rotations happening within one set of images.

- Look at the rotations in the inner and outer segments of this shape.

   The outer segments have rotated 90° clockwise, but the inner segments have rotated 90° anticlockwise.

   Sometimes a second rotation is shown with a shape going around the shaded shape, but it's not very common.

TRY IT OUT

Fresh air

Many local playgrounds and parks have roundabouts that are broken up into sections. If your local park has a roundabout you can use it to help with rotations.

- Go to the park with two friends.
- Get your friends to stand in different segments (but not opposite each other).
- Guess where they will be after a quarter or half turn.
- Who can get it right most often?

TEST YOURSELF

Which of the five boxes on the right completes the sequence on the left? Circle the letter under the box that you think is the correct answer.

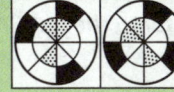

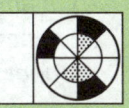

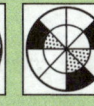

a   b   c   d   e

Rotations

43

3 Improve your skills

Spotting patterns could be the simplest description of non-verbal reasoning. In this section you'll be looking at questions in *grid layouts*. You'll need to identify the *patterns* and continue them to find the answer.

The trick to doing these questions is to look at the images twice; once to see the overall image and a second time to look at the details. Speed might be useful, but **understanding** what you are seeing is **essential**.

What to expect

Spotting patterns questions will always have at least two changes and often more, so make sure you look at all of the images twice as it can be easy to miss something.

The changes can be any connections, from size to shading, from number of shapes to number of lines. Reflections are one of the most common connections in grids as the layout can make them quite clear to see.

In small grids, changes can go along the rows and down the columns.

In large grids, changes can also go diagonally or use the whole grid.

Skills in spotting patterns

Simple shape questions

The simplest questions will show you a shape that changes its 'size' or its 'shading pattern'. You will then be asked to copy that change to a different shape. Other changes you may see include…

- position – moving from one corner to another
- rotation – twisting a quarter turn or half turn
- reflection.

   Simple shape changes will always have just one or two changes and will not have any distractions.

Changing numbers of items

More items are added in the next step on from simple shapes:

- An identical shape could be added.
- A corner may be added to the shape.
- The number of shapes in the box could double.

   Often there are questions where the number of items increases, but sometimes the number decreases – let's be honest, it's just swapping the pictures around!

Spotting patterns

Combination of shapes

In some questions lots of shapes are put together as one item – let's call it a 'compound shape'. They may even end up looking like something that you recognise, such as a car or a boat. Here are some of the changes that the question writer can use in a shape like this:

- the colour of the car body
- the colour of the roof
- the colour of the windscreen strip
- the colour of the headlights, so that they seem to be on or off
- the shape of the headlights
- the whole shape can also be reflected, but the only thing that will appear to move is the steering wheel.

These compound shapes allow the question writer to put lots of changes into a question so that they are less obvious.

Interpreting the changes

Identifying the changes is only half of the question. You then have to apply those changes to a completely different shape. Here's how some of the changes for the car shape could be applied to the boat:

- The car body can be the hull of the boat.

- The car roof can be the sail.

- The boat can be reflected, but this time the difference will be in the sail.

As you can see, the boat shape is not as versatile as the car, but if there were portholes on the boat they could match the headlights.

Sometimes the limitations of one compound shape can be useful as it reduces the number of possible changes.

What you will learn

In this section you will learn:

- how to spot the patterns in grid questions

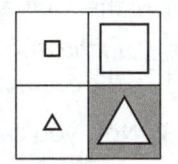

- how to work out what the question is asking you to do

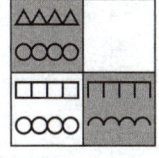

- how to apply changes from one shape to another.

TIPS FOR SUCCESS

Spot the difference

You use these skills whenever you look for changes in a picture. Spot the difference puzzles are a great way to practise looking for small changes, so try to have a go at a few of them. You could even create some for your friends and family to try – see if you can outwit them!

Introducing spotting patterns

45

Simple 2 × 2 grids

3 Improve your skills

2 × 2 grids are similar to *the changing shapes* questions on pages 32–33, just with a different layout. There will always be at least two changes in these problems – one in the rows and one in the columns.

The trick to doing these questions is to spot which of the completed squares are related to each other, what has changed and what has stayed the same. Once you've done that you can see what should fill the empty square.

Understanding 2 × 2 grids

Here are some of the possible changes that are used in 2 × 2 grid questions:

| size | shading | number of shapes |
| rotation | reflection | number of sides or corners |

You will often see a combination of these changes in a row or column. Don't assume that the first thing you spot is all that is happening.

You use these choosing and selecting skills when you are deciding which cake or sweet to take from a box. For example, in this picture you can easily pick out a cake with a cherry on top. You can also pick out a bigger cake.

Simple 2 × 2 grid skills

Grids with simple changes

1. Look closely at this grid. Three of the boxes have a shape in them and one is empty. Think of the three completed boxes as if they make an L shape. It might be on its side or upside down, but it's there.

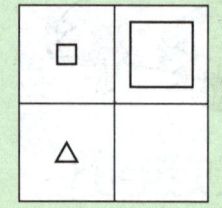

   - Which box is in the **corner of the L**? The patterns are always in rows or columns, so the shape in this box is the key to getting the answer.
     In this grid, the top left box with the small square is in the corner of the L.

2. Now you can look for similarities in both of the other filled boxes.
   - Next to the small square is a big square. Underneath the small square is a small triangle. What is changing in the rows and columns?
     In the rows it's the size that changes. In the columns it's the shape that changes.

3. Now you can put the two rules together.

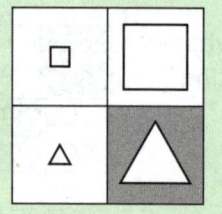

   - What is the missing shape?
     The shape that fits the empty box must be a different size (row change) and a different shape (column change). It must be a bigger triangle.

Spotting patterns

Simple 2 × 2 grids

Skills in changing one question into another

2 × 2 grid and changing shapes (or 'pairs') questions on pages 32–33 both use the same skills. Both have three filled boxes and one empty box that must be filled. If you find one way of doing these questions difficult, try changing the question into the other style. You can do this in your head or by sketching beside the question.

Changing 'pairs' into a 2 × 2 grid

With changing shapes questions you are given three boxes.

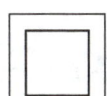

- The first box should become the corner of your L, and go in the top left box of the 2 × 2 grid.
- The second box is the pair for the first one. It should go in the top right box.
- The third box should go in the bottom left box.

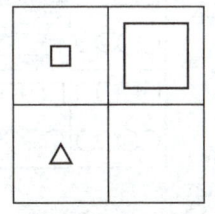

To fill the grid you can work out what is in the bottom right box by following the same procedure as before.

Changing a 2 × 2 grid into pairs

With the 2 × 2 grid question you are given three boxes.

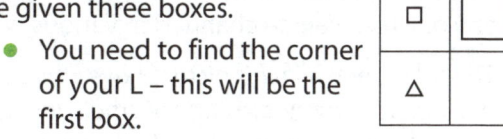

- You need to find the corner of your L – this will be the first box.
- Look at the two remaining boxes. Whichever looks the most similar should be the next box. These two boxes make up the first pair.
- The remaining box is the first shape of the second pair.

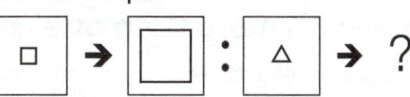

You need to work out what goes in the fourth (or last) box to complete the second pair.

TRY IT OUT
Play time

Play a game with your friends to see who is the quickest to spot the patterns in a group of toys.

- Make a grid of four toys or games: perhaps teddy bears or balls of different sizes or colours.
- Try making up two patterns such as increasing sizes or type of toy. You can even pair them up in the grid to make it harder.
- The first person to guess the pattern gets to pick the game you'll play next.

TEST YOURSELF

Which of the boxes on the right can be used to complete the grid on the left? Circle the letter under the box that you think is the correct answer.

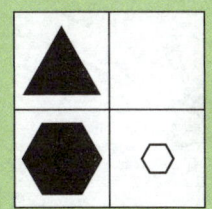

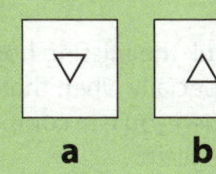

a   b   c   d   e

3 Improve your skills

Understanding more complex 2 × 2 grids

In some questions the changes are more difficult to spot. There can be more than one change to both the rows and the columns. Sometimes each box in the grid contains several simple shapes, any of which can be changed in various ways.

The cakes shown in this picture have white or pink icing, are with or without a cherry, are large or small and have plain or patterned cases. You can work out the rules for what changes across the rows and what changes down the columns.

Complex 2 × 2 grid skills

Grids with more than one change in a row or column

1. Begin in exactly the same way as you did for the previous example – finding the corner of the L.

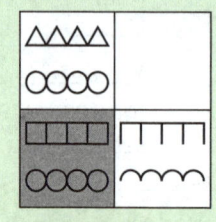

   - Which box is in the corner of the L?
   For this grid, it's the bottom left box.

   The box has four squares side by side above four circles.

2. Now look at what's in the other boxes.

   - There are the same four circles but with four triangles in the box above. There are four semicircles and what looks like the squares but without the baselines in the box to the right. What is changing in the rows and columns?

   There are changes to the shapes in both directions. In the columns the top shape has changed from squares to triangles. In the rows there are two things happening: the circles and the squares have both been altered.

3. Look carefully at the changes to the shapes in the rows.

   - In the bottom right box, the circles have been cut in half to make semicircles. The squares in the same box have lost their baselines. What should go in the missing box?

   To create the shape in the empty top right box you need to do the same. Cut the circles in half and remove the baselines from the triangles to create a zig-zag pattern.

TIPS FOR SUCCESS

Sketch

It's often easier to work out what you think the missing box should contain by sketching inside it, especially when there's more than one change to think about. Then you can compare it with the possible answers you've been given.

Spotting patterns

More complex 2 x 2 grids

Trickier changes

1. Once again, begin in exactly the same way as you did for the previous examples – finding the corner of the L.
   - Which box is the corner of the L?

   For this grid, it's the bottom right box.

2. The box has what looks like a sailing boat on the waves, with a sun in the sky. There are lots of shapes in there, but they look like something else, so you can use the 'picture' you can see to help you spot the changes. Look at what's in the other boxes.
   - In the box above the boat you can see what looks like a car with the same sun in the sky.
   - In the box to the left is the sailing boat on the sea again. This time the boat is black and it's been reflected in the line between the boxes. The sun has become a moon and has also swapped sides.
   - What types of changes have been made?

   This question contains 'reflections', 'colour changes' and 'shape changes'. You need to look at these changes one step at a time.

3. Look at the top right box to see how it can be turned it into a shape for the empty box.
   - What changes will you need to make?

   First you need to reflect the car – the steering wheel needs to move sides. 

   Now the colour of the car body and roof needs to change. 

   Finally, the sun will need to change into a moon and move to the other side of the box. 

   The missing box is a reflected black car at night. 

   - Even in these sorts of grid questions you will find some distractions.

   In this example the waves the boat is sitting on are not represented in the image for the car, just as the car headlights are not on the boat.

TEST YOURSELF

Which of the boxes on the right can be used to complete the grid on the left? Circle the letter under the box that you think is the correct answer.

1.

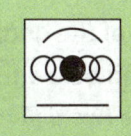

   a   b   c   d   e

2.

   a   b   c   d   e

49

Simple 3 × 3 grids

3 Improve your skills

3 × 3 grids are the next step on from the 2 × 2 grids. There is often more than one rule to follow in these problems and you need to be able to exclude things that are put there to distract you.

The trick to doing these questions is to look at how each square relates to the ones around it, even those that just touch on the corners.

Understanding 3 × 3 grids

Here are some of the possible changes that are used in 3 × 3 grids:

- size
- shading
- number of shapes
- rotation
- reflection
- number of sides or corners

There will be a combination of these changes in a 3 × 3 grid. Some changes will go across the rows and some changes will go down the columns or across the diagonals. You need to look for the different patterns these changes make.

At the seaside you can choose to have a small, medium or large ice-cream, with or without hundreds and thousands or a flake. The 3 × 3 grid here shows you the choices available and how each one relates to those around it.

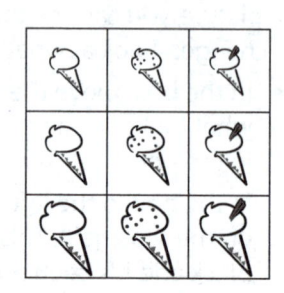

Skills in 3 × 3 grids

Grids with a simple change

1. One of the best places to start to look for patterns is with the **top square** of the **middle column**.

   - The shape in the top square of the middle column is a circle. To the left is a square and to the right is a triangle.

     None of the 'shapes' are the same in this row, but they are the same 'size'. You will need to look at other areas of the grid to see if there are any further similarities or patterns.

2. If you cannot find a pattern across the 'rows' of the grid, try looking down the 'columns'.

   - Below the circle is a slightly bigger circle and below that circle is an even bigger circle.

     The matching shapes and increasing sizes are two different possible patterns.

3. Once you have spotted a pattern or patterns, you need to check the other columns in the grid to see if these patterns are repeated.

   - The first column is made up of a square that gets bigger and bigger. The last column is made up of two triangles; the lower one is larger than the top one.

     The shape that fits the empty box must be a bigger triangle, to match the pattern of the other columns. It must also be the same size as the square and circle in that row.

50

Spotting patterns

Simple 3 × 3 grids

Grids with a reflection

1 Sometimes 3 × 3 grid questions will have a reflection pattern in them. They don't always just reflect one box into the next. The line of symmetry can go through the centre of the middle row or column.

- This sort of question will often have lots of shapes in each box, although you'll sometimes see only one in the row or column which has the line of symmetry going through it.

There is just one shape in the middle column here. This will usually mean that the pattern is symmetrical.

2 If you think the question is about symmetry, look for boxes that contain similar shapes.

- In this grid, both the light grey squares have a heart and a right-angled triangle in them.
- Both the darker squares have a pentagon and a hexagon in them.

Remember that reflection means some shapes, for example the right-angled triangle, will look different.

3 Once you have spotted the symmetrical pattern, it's often a good idea to mark the line of symmetry on the question. It can be done quickly and doesn't need to be accurate as it's just there to help you think about the reflected shapes.

- You should now be able to work out what should go into the empty box. In this grid it's a reflection of the top left box.

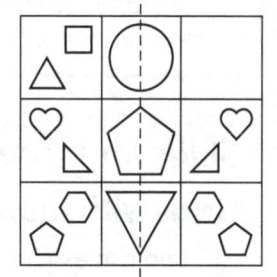

It will be a square and a triangle. The square is in the top left corner of the box and the triangle is in the bottom right corner.

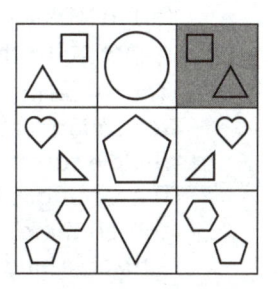

TEST YOURSELF

Which of the boxes on the right can be used to complete the grid on the left? Circle the letter under the box that you think is the correct answer.

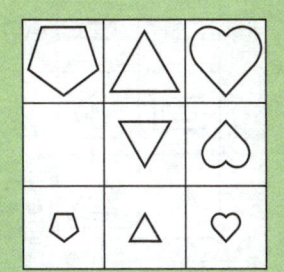

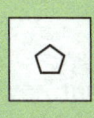

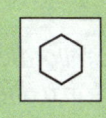

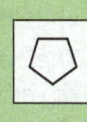

a   b   c   d   e

3 Improve your skills

Understanding more complex 3 × 3 grids

The patterns in some grids can be more difficult to spot. The changes can be more complicated or they can go along diagonals rather than down columns or across rows. Working methodically will help you find the patterns so that you can complete the grid.

Variations in the choice of lolly, cone and tub available at the seaside are shown in this grid. You can see patterns for the different choices.

Skills for more complex 3 × 3 grids

Grids with more than one change

1. Begin in exactly the same way as you did for the grids with a simple change: start to look for patterns with the **top square** of the **middle column**.

   - The shape in the top square of the middle column is a rectangle. To the left there's a triangle, and to the right a pentagon.

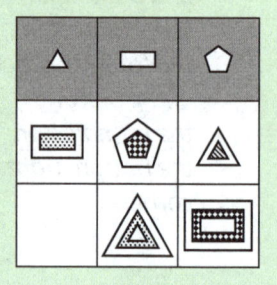

   The shapes are all different in this row, but they all have black outlines and no shading. You will need to look at other areas of the grid for further similarities and patterns.

2. If you cannot find a pattern across the rows of the grid, try looking down the columns.

   - In the box below the rectangle are two pentagons, one inside the other. The inner one has a pattern on it that looks a bit like a chessboard.

   There are no obvious similarities here, so you will need to look in a different direction again.

3. Patterns often appear diagonally on 3 × 3 grids so this is the next direction to look in.

   - In the box below and to the left of the rectangle there are two rectangles, one inside the other. The inner rectangle has a pattern on it but is different to the pattern on the pentagon – it's made up of small dots.

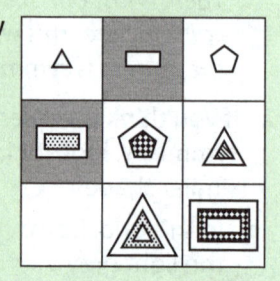

   Even though the match doesn't seem to be exact, it is worth looking at other diagonals to see if there are any other clues to the pattern.

4. There are three possible diagonal patterns going down and left in a 3 × 3 grid, and three more going down and right. It is worth looking at all of these when you are trying to find these patterns.

   - The box at the bottom right of the grid is also a rectangle (following the same diagonal pattern as the other rectangles), although this

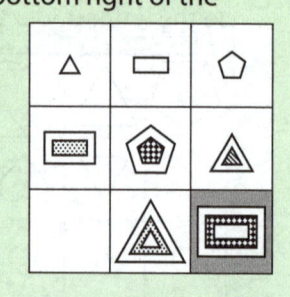

52

Spotting patterns

box has **three** rectangles, one inside another, and the middle one has a chessboard pattern on it.

Each time you go down a row, the shape moves one column to the left and a similar shape is added inside it. However, this doesn't explain the shading pattern.

5 Once you are satisfied that you have identified one pattern, move on to work out any others that you have spotted.

- The pentagons in the centre box and the rectangles in the bottom right box feature a chessboard pattern. The rectangles in the middle row have a dotted pattern. The triangles in the bottom row also have a dotted pattern.

The patterns move across to the right as you progress down the rows. The triangles in the middle row have a diagonal striped pattern, which must be used in the missing shape.

So, putting everything together, the missing shape must be three pentagons – one inside another, and the second one should have a diagonal striped pattern.

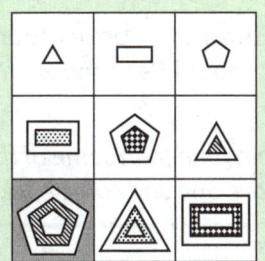

TRY IT OUT
Sweet treat

Play a game with your friends to see who is the quickest to spot a pattern in a tray of sweets.

- Make a grid of nine sweets – chocolate mint or orange sticks work well as you can break them into different lengths.
- Try making up a pattern such as increasing sizes or different angles. You can even overlap them to make crosses or shapes such as squares and triangles.
- The first person to guess the pattern gets to eat the sweets!

More complex 3 × 3 grids

TEST YOURSELF

Which of the boxes on the right can be used to complete the grid on the left? Circle the letter under the box that you think is the correct answer.

1

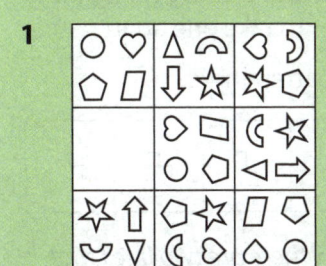

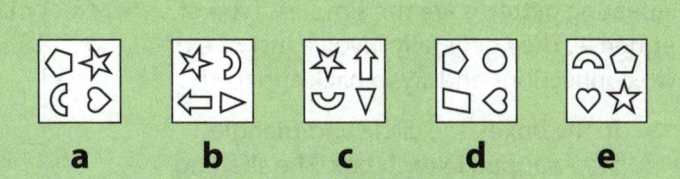

2

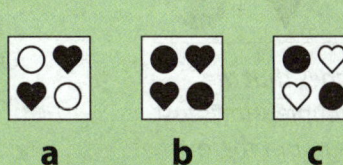

a   b   c   d   e

a   b   c   d   e

53

3 Improve your skills

Completing sequences is about finding the story behind the changes, even when that story might be slightly hidden.

The trick to doing these questions is to find the differences between the images. If that isn't telling you the whole story, look for the differences between the differences. The number of shapes may increase each time, but you may have to add an extra two shapes to the increase each time.

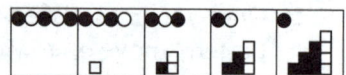

What to expect

Sequences can use all of the **connections** and **relationships** you've already seen, but there are different types of sequences:

- **repeating patterns**
- **one-step patterns**
- **two-step patterns**
- **number patterns**

Although there are four different types of sequence, you'll be using the same skills to look for what changes and what stays the same.

In all of these questions you'll be shown five boxes, four with images in and one blank box. You'll need to work out what should be in the empty box and pick it from the five possible answers you are given.

These questions will take a little more time than some of the others. Try not to rush them, but don't be afraid to leave one and come back to it at the end.

Different sequences and patterns

In each of the examples there is no empty box for an answer; this is to help you see the whole pattern at this stage.

Repeating patterns

Repeating patterns are the simplest type of sequence. They generally involve just one or two connections and swap back and forth.

- In the boxes, the circle and triangle are swapped in each box. The shading stays the same each time.

Here there are two images that are swapped over. This example shows just one shape in each image, but there could be two or more.

One-step patterns

Often in one-step patterns the same connection happens over and over again to build up a shape or to take one apart.

- What is the pattern here?

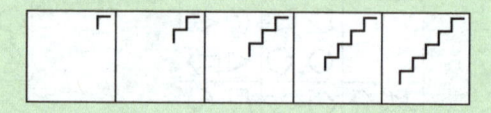

In the first box there are two lines that are joined together to make a right angle.

In each box, two more lines are added to create a string of right angles – it almost looks like a staircase.

Completing sequences

Two-step patterns

In two-step patterns there are usually two changes happening. You can also see shapes being built up.

- Can you spot the sequence here?

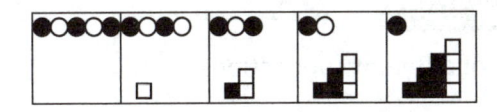

In this example, one circle is removed from the row at the top, and it's always removed from the right-hand end.

One column of white squares is added that is one square higher than the previous column.

The previous squares are then turned black.

The size of the circles doesn't change, nor does the size of the squares.

There are no squares in the first box. This is not unusual as it's a great distraction. You need to look at all the boxes to get a good idea of the patterns.

Number patterns

There is a range of different number patterns. Here's one of the simpler ones.

- Can you tell what is happening?

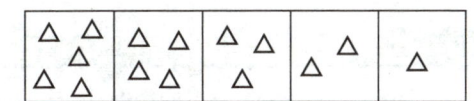

In each box there is one less triangle than the previous box.

Number patterns can involve sequences of numbers that you've probably used in the past, such as square numbers. It does mean the boxes can get a little crowded!

TIPS FOR SUCCESS

Layers

In most of the patterns you've seen so far, the changes have been right in front of you, even if they've been rather subtle. Now you need to look a little deeper. If the changes are not the same, you need to go down to the next layer in the puzzle and compare what is happening with the changes to find the pattern.

What you will learn

In this section you will learn:

- how to spot repeating patterns

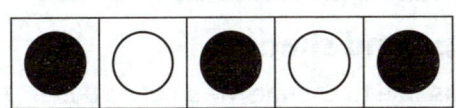

- how to spot one-step patterns

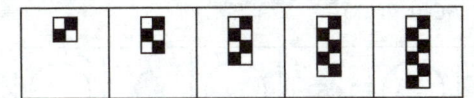

- how to spot two-step patterns

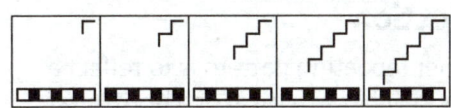

- how to spot a range of number patterns.

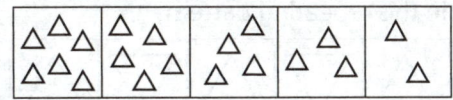

Introducing completing sequences

3 Improve your skills

Repeating patterns are the building blocks of sequences. If the pattern doesn't repeat, it's not really a sequence.

The changes may be simple, such as adding a single small shape each step, or they may be complicated, such as changing shapes and rotating them.

Understanding repeating patterns

Repeating patterns can be built up from a number of different connections and relationships including:

number of shapes	number of lines	number of corners
size	shape	shading
rotation	reflection	

Repeating patterns make the same basic changes in every step. The pattern could be that one shape swaps to another and back again, or that the shading pattern swaps each time.

Some of these questions will seem to be obvious, but remember to take a few moments to look twice at each question just to be sure.

Skills for back and forth patterns

In these questions you simply have two images that keep swapping.

Shapes

When a pattern involves two shapes that swap, the change should be obvious.

- What is the repeating pattern shown here?

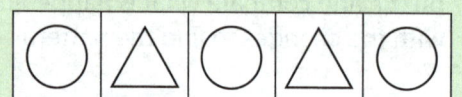

○ △ ○ △ ○

The shape keeps swapping between a circle and a triangle, but nothing else is changing.

Reflection

Another repeating pattern is to reflect a shape in either a vertical or a horizontal mirror line and back again.

- What type of mirror line is being used in this repeating pattern?

△ ▽ △ ▽ △

The triangle is being reflected in a horizontal mirror line.

Shading

Sometimes a repeating pattern can be the shading of a shape swapping back and forth.

- What change is made each time to give this repeating pattern?

● ○ ● ○ ●

The shape is always a circle but the shading swaps each time.

Shape and shading

It's possible to change the shading *and* the shape.

- What is the repeating pattern in this sequence?

○ ▲ ○ ▲ ○

The pattern swaps between a white circle and a shaded triangle each time.

Completing sequences

Skills for building up patterns

In these questions the repeated pattern is used to add shapes to build a shape.

A basic build

A simple repeating pattern is built up.

- Look at this sequence.

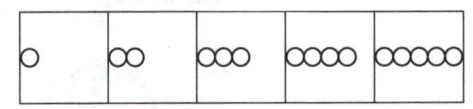

One circle is added in each box to the right of the previous circle.

A build with more elements

More elements are changed at a time to build up a more complex repeating pattern.

- Have a look at these five boxes and see if you can describe what's going on.

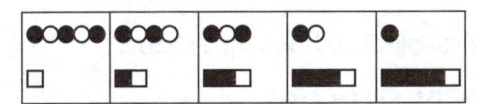

There is one less circle in each box. Each time the circle on the right is removed.

A white square is added in each box, and any existing squares turn black.

TRY IT OUT

Hands up!

You can look at a simple repeating pattern at any time.

- Hold your hand up so that you are looking at your palm.
- Turn your hand around so that you are looking at the back of your hand.
- Turn it back to the palm, then to the back, and keep repeating.

TIPS FOR SUCCESS

Noughts and crosses

If you are finding it difficult to spot the repeating pattern, take two of the boxes that are next to each other and put a spot or a cross over the bits that are in both. Whatever changes will not have a mark on it.

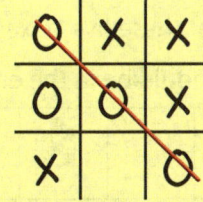

TEST YOURSELF

Which of the images on the right can be used to complete the sequence in the boxes on the left? Circle the letter under the box that you think is the correct answer.

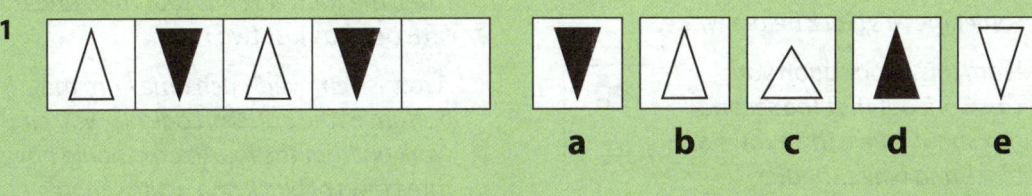

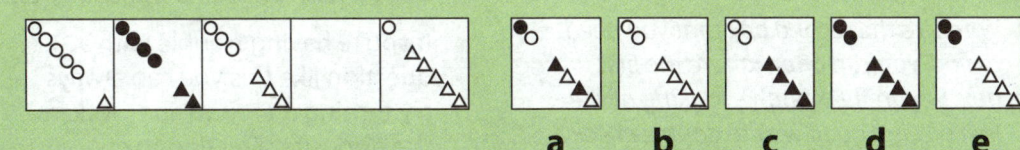

1

2

3 Improve your skills

One-step patterns are the building blocks of shapes and sequences. In these questions you'll see the same change happen in each box in the sequence.

The changes may be simple, but there will always be just one. Once you've identified the change, you know what is happening.

Understanding one-step patterns

One-step patterns can use any of the following connections:

| number of shapes | size | shape |
| shading | rotation | |

Size is slightly less common, as getting five similar shapes of different sizes can be tricky as the boxes are so small.

One-step patterns are similar to building a wall out of identical bricks. You always add one brick at a time of the same size.

Skills for building a shape

In these questions you simply keep adding an identical block to build up a shape.

Construction

Have a look at these five boxes.

- What should be in the empty one?

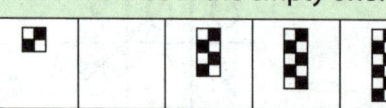

The first box has two rows of black and white squares, the third box has four rows, the fourth box has five rows and the fifth box has six rows.

A row is 'added' each time at the bottom to continue the pattern, so sometimes the pattern is white before black and sometimes it's black before white.

From this information you can work out that the second box should have three rows of black and white squares.

When it's the second box that you need to find, you can often ignore the first box. Be careful though – looking at the first box is a good way to double check your answer.

Deconstruction

Some questions are the other way round to construction questions. The sequence will look like you are *removing* the same piece each time.

- Here is the same question that you've just looked at, but the boxes have been reversed.

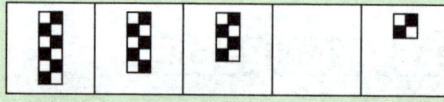

The first box has six rows of black and white squares, the second box has five rows, the third box has four rows and the fifth box has just two rows.

A row is 'removed' each time from the bottom of the pattern. Logically, you can work out that the fourth box should have three rows of black and white squares.

- If you're having trouble with a question like this you can always try turning it around and work in the opposite direction to give you a different view of it.

Completing sequences

One-step patterns

Skills for rotation

A rotating shape can be used in a question. A simple rotation can be a one-step pattern.

- In this example you can see a 90° clockwise rotation.

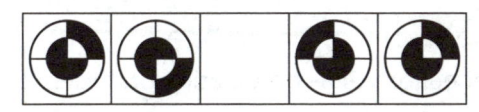

The whole shape is rotating as one, so it's a one-step pattern.

Skills for moving a shape

In another sort of one-step pattern, a shape moves round inside the boxes.

- Have a look at these five boxes. Can you see what is happening?

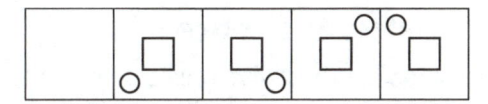

Every box has a square and a circle in it.

The square does not move or change in any way (it's a distraction).

The circle moves from one corner to another in an anticlockwise direction.

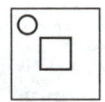

The empty box should have a circle in the top left corner, just like the fifth box.

This is another sort of rotation, although often the shape will remain the same way up. Remember that when you've got a 90° rotation, the last box and the first box will often be the same.

TRY IT OUT
Onion skin

Cartoon animators used to check that they were drawing in the right place by using the 'onion skin' technique. They would finish one animation cell, and once it was dry they'd put another one on top and draw on it so they could see what they had already done. That way characters such as Snow White didn't jump from one side of the screen to the other and back again several times a second.

- Use the onion skin technique with tracing paper to build up your own sequences.
- Take one picture out of the sequence and see if your friends can work out the missing picture.
- Can you work out the missing picture when they try the onion skin technique on you?

TIPS FOR SUCCESS
Focus

When you are looking at a question that may be a one-step pattern, you should focus on two boxes that are beside each other. Work out the changes and then check that the same change will give you the next box. If that's the empty box, add the change again and see if it matches the next box. Just remember that sometimes you'll be working backwards and have to remove items, especially if it's the first box that you've got to find.

TEST YOURSELF

Which of the images on the right can be used to complete the sequence in the boxes on the left? Circle the letter under the box that you think is the correct answer.

a b c d e

3 Improve your skills

Two-step patterns have two different patterns going on at the same time.

These questions will have two or more changes. The changes might be similar, such as removing one shape while adding another, or completely different, such as rotating the shape and changing the shading.

Understanding two-step patterns

Two-step patterns can use any of the following connections or a combination of these:

| number of shapes | size | shape |
| shading | rotation | reflection |

Reflection can be paired up with anything to give a two-step pattern. Reflection by itself is a repeating pattern.

Two-step patterns are a bit like walking. You've got to move one foot first then the other before you can move the first foot again.

Skills for building shapes

Combination of shapes

Some questions will test your observation skills by changing one shape for another in the same way.

- What is happening in this pattern?

Each box has seven shapes, and after the first box, those shapes are made up of a mixture of squares and circles.

The first box has seven squares, the second box has six squares and one circle, the third box has five squares and two circles, the fourth box is the one you are trying to find and the last one has three squares and four circles.

The pattern is that one of the squares is removed and a circle is added in each box. The empty box should have four squares and three circles.

This may look like a one-step pattern as it's a replacement, but if you think of it as removing one thing and adding something else, you have two different actions taking place.

Two patterns at once

Have a look at these five boxes.

- What should be in the empty one?

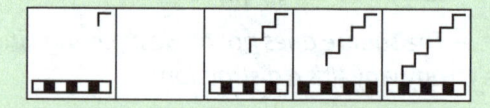

The first box has two lines in the top right corner, joined together to make a right angle. It also has seven squares at the bottom that alternate between black and white.

The third box has three sets of the lines at right angles and the same seven squares at the bottom. Does that mean the empty box should have two sets of lines and the same squares?

No, it doesn't. There are two boxes you've not looked at yet and the fourth one shows that the squares swap between black and white before swapping back for the fifth box.

The correct answer is two sets of lines with seven black and white squares, starting with a black square.

Completing sequences

Skills for two repeating patterns

Some questions will show you two repeating patterns that overlap each other.

- Have a look at these five boxes and try to describe what's going on.

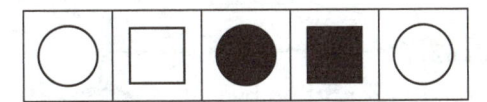

The shapes swap between a circle and a square.

The first circle and square are white, the second circle and square are black. The last circle is also white.

There are two repeating patterns – one pattern changing the shape, and one pattern changing the colour.

It looks quite unusual, but is the sort of question you may see.

TRY IT OUT
Footprints

Try creating your own two-step pattern with your feet.

- You can create a pattern on the sand either at the beach or using water from a puddle on your wellies.
- Take one step with each foot in one direction. Turn left and take another two steps, then turn right and start again.

Skills for reversing patterns

1. Some patterns seem to reverse part way through.

   - Have a look at this complete pattern

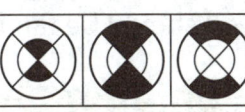

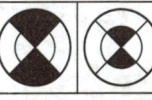

   The shading seems to spread out from the middle, into the outer segments in the first few boxes. Once it's only in the outer segments, it reverses and heads back towards the middle again.

2. Shading is the most common connection in this sort of question as it can be made to look complicated when it's actually fairly easy.

   - The simplest example of this sort of question is one where a single shape changes. Look at this complete pattern.

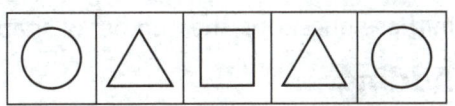

   The circle changes into a triangle and then a square. After that the pattern reverses and the square becomes a triangle and a circle once more.

   - Something to watch out for with this sort of question is that you can put a vertical mirror line down the middle of the centre shape and both sides will look the same.

   This sort of question can often have rotation as a second pattern, so keep an eye out for other connections and patterns when you see a question like this. Unfortunately, that means there can be distractions as well.

TEST YOURSELF

Which of the images on the right can be used to complete the sequence in the boxes on the left? Circle the letter under the box that you think is the correct answer.

a   b   c   d   e

Two-step patterns

61

3 Improve your skills

Number patterns bring a little bit of adding, subtracting and multiplying into questions on sequences.

Rather than digits, you'll see the number of shapes changing by a rule, such as adding one or maybe doubling the number each time. Some changes will follow a pattern you should be familiar with, such as square numbers.

Understanding number patterns

Number patterns will often change by a fixed number or proportion by…

- adding the same number
- subtracting the same number
- multiplying by the same number

The total number of items is limited by the size of the boxes, so there shouldn't be more than 25 items in the box that has the most items.

Adding or subtracting two shapes each time will give you the sequence of odd or even numbers, depending on what you started with.

Skills for fixed number changes

In these questions, the number of shapes changes by the *same amount* each time.

Adding

Have a look at these five boxes.

- Can you work out what should be in the middle one?

You can see that the same shape is in each box a different number of times, so the first thing to do is count the shapes.

The first box has one circle, the second has three, the third you have to work out, the fourth has seven and the last has nine.

The difference between the first and second box is two, and the difference between the fourth and fifth boxes is two.

Now that you've got a possible rule, it's best to check if it works. The second box has three circles, so adding two more will give you five. If you add two more to go to the fourth box you get seven, which you know is correct.

Don't worry about remembering how many are in each box – just write a number above or below the box.

TRY IT OUT

Counting in groups

You're probably used to working out your four times table by reciting the answers: 4, 8, 12, 16, 20…

- What do you do if you need to count in fours starting from six?

- Pick a number to add on each time and pick a single digit number that isn't in that times table to start from. See how quickly you can get past 25.
- Try it with your friends and set each other challenges to see who is quickest.

62

Simple number patterns

Spotting patterns

Subtracting

Subtraction is the opposite of addition. In questions on number patterns, subtraction is the same question as addition, just with the boxes in reverse order.

- Have a look at these five boxes and see if you can work out what's going on.

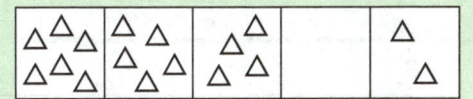

Once again, you've got the same shape in each box.

The first box has six triangles, the second box has five, the third has four, the fourth box is the one you are trying to work out and the last box has two triangles in it.

Having three filled boxes in a row does make it a little easier as you can see the pattern more easily. The number of triangles goes down by one in each box. That means the empty box should have three triangles in it.

If you find addition easier than subtraction you can always work from the right rather than the left.

Multiplying

Multiplying is something you'll see every now and then. Generally it will be limited to the two or three times table, if only because of how little space there is in the boxes.

- What number pattern can you find in these five boxes?

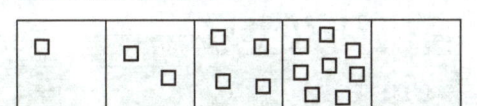

Once again, you've got the same shape in each box.

The first box has one square in it, the second has two, the third has four and the fourth has eight. The fifth box is the one you need to work out.

The gap between the first two boxes is one, between the second and third boxes it's two, and between the third and fourth boxes it's four.

The number of squares in each box is doubling each time, so there should be 16 squares in the last box.

TEST YOURSELF

Which of the images on the right can be used to complete the sequence in the boxes on the left? Circle the letter under the box that you think is the correct answer.

1.   a b c d e

2.   a b c d e

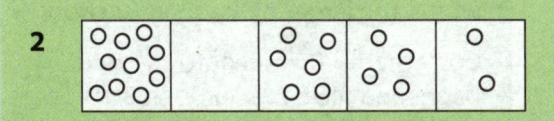

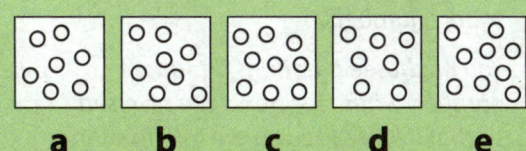

3 Improve your skills

Understanding more complex number patterns

Questions on number patterns can also change by following a pattern you might recognise, such as…

square numbers   **triangular numbers**

The total number of items is limited by the size of the boxes, so there shouldn't be more than 25 items in the box that has the most items.

Adding or subtracting two shapes each time will give you the sequence of odd or even numbers, depending on what you started with.

Skills for square numbers

When you multiply a number by itself, the answer is a square number. The name comes from the way you can lay out the numbers from one to the square number in a square grid, with one number in each box.

Questions with square numbers

Square number questions rely on you remembering the first five or six square numbers.

- Look at these five boxes. Can you spot the number pattern?

You can see that the same shape is in each box a different number of times, so the first thing to do is count the shapes.

The first box has one circle, the second has four, the third box has nine, the fourth has 16 and the last you have to work out.

The number added in each box also varies – it's always odd and increases by two each time.

Using this information you can work out that there should be 25 circles in the empty box, but it is quicker if you spot the square numbers.

You might see questions on square numbers where the boxes are reversed, so that it looks like you are taking shapes out of the box each time.

TRY IT OUT

Patterns

Look at this completed section of the square number grid. The grid is colour-coded so that you can see how the square numbers are formed.

As you can see, all the numbers from one to the square number fit into the large square it sits in on the grid. For example, all the numbers 1–9 fit within the larger pink square section.

Copy the 1–100 grid onto squared paper and fill in the numbers so that every number that is less than the square number is inside the square section of the grid it relates to.

Completing sequences

Skills for triangular numbers

Triangular numbers are a sequence made up by adding whole numbers together. If you want the fifth triangular number you have to add together all of the numbers from one to five.

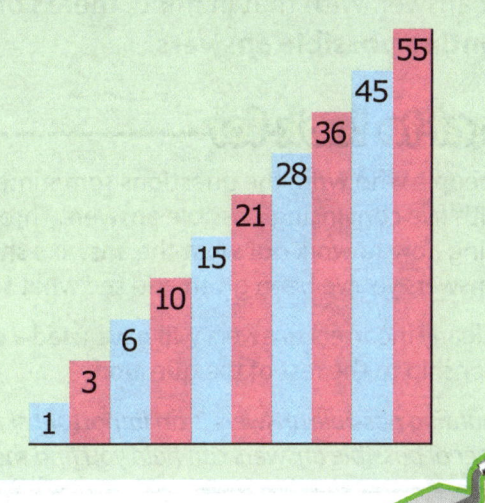

1
1 + 2 = 3
1 + 2 + 3 = 6
1 + 2 + 3 + 4 = 10
1 + 2 + 3 + 4 + 5 = 15
1 + 2 + 3 + 4 + 5 + 6 = 21
1 + 2 + 3 + 4 + 5 + 6 + 7 = 28

Questions with triangular numbers

Have a look at these five boxes.

- What is happening to the shapes?

  You can see that the same shape is in each box a different number of times, so the first thing to do is count the shapes.

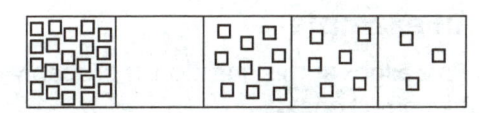

The first box has 21 squares, the second is the one you have to work out, the third box has 10 squares, the fourth has six and the last has three.

This time the number of shapes is decreasing.

The difference between the third and fourth boxes is four, and between the last two boxes it is three. It looks like the gap goes down by one each time – the gaps are consecutive numbers.

The difference between the first and third boxes is eleven. What two consecutive numbers can be added together to get eleven? The answer is five and six.

Using that information you can work out that there should be six less than 21 squares in the empty box, or five more than 10. Working both of those out comes to 15.

You probably expected that one of the boxes would have just one shape in it as the first triangular number is one.

TEST YOURSELF

Which of the images on the right can be used to complete the sequence in the boxes on the left? Circle the letter under the box that you think is the correct answer.

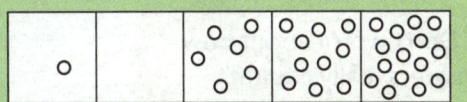

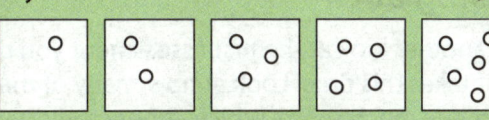

a   b   c   d   e

Square and triangular number patterns

65

3 Improve your skills: Non-verbal reasoning essentials

Non-verbal reasoning has lots of different types of questions which all require similar skills of observation and consideration.

Sometimes you'll look at a question and find it difficult to work out the correct answer. With that in mind, there's one more skill to look at – **discounting possible answers**.

What to look for

The people who write the questions sometimes find that it's difficult to come up with five convincing possible answers. Throughout this book you've been learning how to work out what the answers should be. Now it's time to look at the answers you've been given and see what simply doesn't fit.

The clearly incorrect answers will have used a different connection or relationship to the rest of the question.

Discounting possible answers is an important skill because reducing the number of possible answers can help you find the correct answer.

Finding the nonsense

An example

Have a look at this question. It probably will not take you long to work out that answer a is the correct one.

- How realistic are the other options?

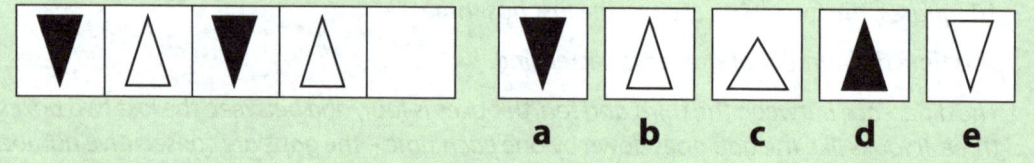

b is seen in the sequence, so that's quite possible.

c is not seen in the sequence at all – it's too short and too wide.

d looks familiar but all of the black triangles point down.

e looks familiar but all of the white triangles point up.

Out of the five possible answers, three can be discounted very quickly.

TIPS FOR SUCCESS

Looking back

Have another look at the first assessment you did. Don't worry about how long it takes this time. Look at how many of the answers really couldn't have made much sense. Which connections have been used to make those answers? Which connections are used regularly for the wrong answers?

Non-verbal reasoning essentials

Nets of a cube

From everything you've seen, you might think that non-verbal reasoning is rather flat as it's all been based around 2-D shapes. With 3-D technology taking off, you're probably interested in some 3-D questions to go with it.

Finding the nets of a cube is a traditional non-verbal reasoning skill, but it's not as common as it used to be.

Understanding nets of a cube

You've probably unfolded a cube in Maths lessons to get a net. You may even know that there are lots of different nets of a cube, depending on how you unfold it.

In non-verbal reasoning, all of the faces of the cube have patterns on them. One might be plain black, one might be striped and one might have circles on it. You might be shown a net and be asked to match it to a cube, or you might be shown a cube and asked to match it to a net.

Although these sorts of questions don't come up that often, it's a good idea to study some patterned cubes and their nets just in case.

Unlocking the cube

An example

Generally, every face on a cube will have a different pattern or shape on it.

- Have a look at this cube. What do you see?
  One face is black, one has stripes on it and one has a single arrow on it.

  You can see these three patterned faces of the cube, but you can't see the other three faces. Once the cube is unfolded to form the net, the three 'unknown' faces will be a distraction.

- Here are the five possible nets. Which is the correct one?

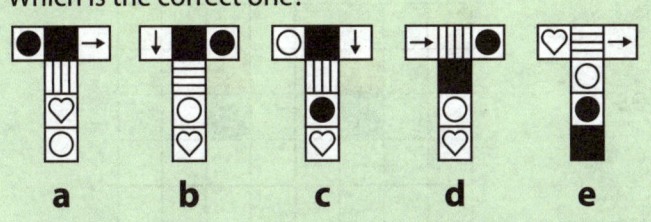

  a   b   c   d   e

  *The answer is **a**. The striped pattern runs into the black square, which means the answer can't be **b** or **e**. Once the net is folded, the arrow will point in the same direction as the striped pattern, which means the answer can't be **c** or **d**. That leaves just **a**.*

TIPS FOR SUCCESS

Practice makes perfect

Non-verbal reasoning is all about the way you think when trying to work out the patterns.

67

3 Improve your skills: Non-verbal reasoning essentials

Complete the activities on the following two pages to help you with the reflection and rotation skills on pages 38–43.

You will need the following equipment to help you with these questions.
- mirror
- tracing paper.

The solutions are on page 81.

Reflective symmetry with one mirror line

Something has reflective symmetry if it looks the same when it is reflected either side of a mirror line. Simple reflections can be vertical, horizontal or diagonal.

In the practice exercises below, place the mirror on the line with the arrow so that it faces the coloured shape. Look at the reflection to see what the symmetrical pattern looks like.

Colour the squares on the opposite side of the mirror line to create the symmetrical shape.

Reflections in vertical lines

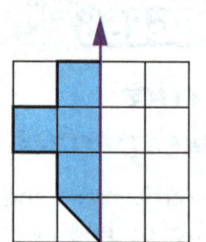

Reflections in horizontal lines

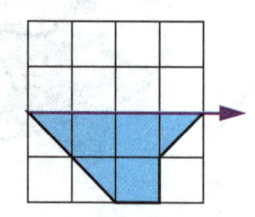

Reflections in diagonal lines

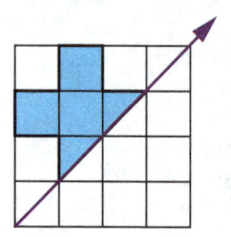

Reflective symmetry with two mirror lines

Sometimes reflections are more complicated and reflect in more than one direction.

Reflections in vertical and horizontal lines

This pattern has reflective symmetry across *both* the vertical and horizontal mirror lines.

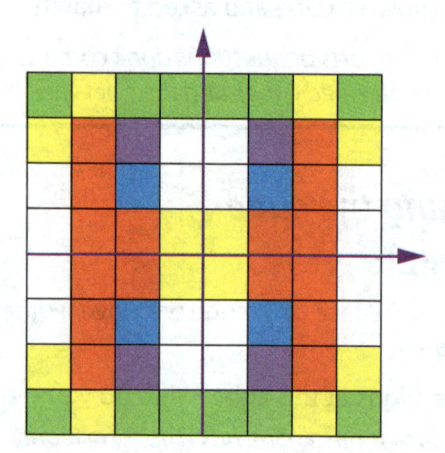

Colour the grid below so that it has reflective symmetry across the vertical and horizontal mirror lines marked with arrows. Once you have completed the pattern, see if you can add to it.

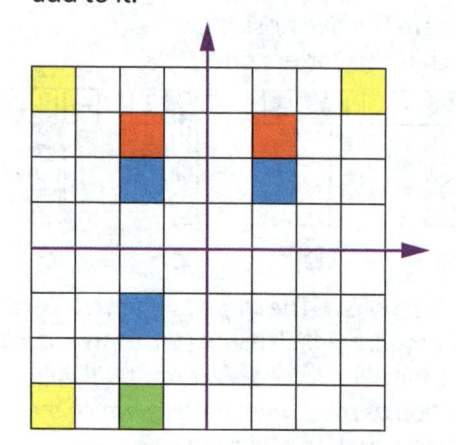

Working with reflections and rotations

Non-verbal reasoning essentials

Reflections in two diagonal lines

Colour the grid below so that it has reflective symmetry across both diagonal mirror lines.

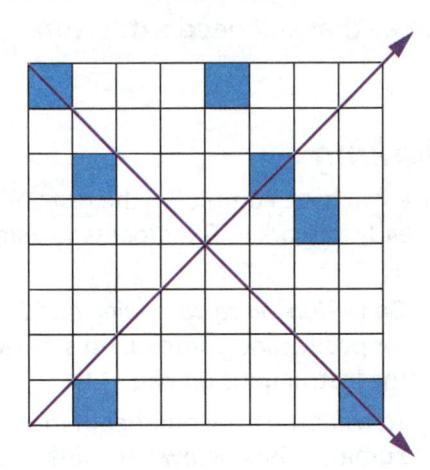

Rotations

A shape has rotational symmetry if it can be turned to fit into its outline in different positions.

Place the tracing paper onto the diamond shape and draw around it. Put a dot in one corner of the shape. Now turn the traced shape around

to see how many times it fits into the original.

As the diamond only fits into the shape in two positions it has a rotational symmetry of **order 2**.

Use tracing paper to find out the rotational symmetry of these shapes.

Working with reflections and rotations

69

4 Test for success

Now you have completed your practice, you are ready to take the second more challenging Practice test.

Non-verbal reasoning test 2 (located in the pull-out booklet) will confirm your ability to answer harder questions and highlight any areas that still need extra work.

Taking the second test

Follow the guidance on page 10 for timing, equipment, surroundings, question types and tips before taking this second test. You should allow **45 minutes** to complete it.

Remember: this is a test to help you to find your strengths and weaknesses. Because of this it is important not to choose a multiple-choice option or guess randomly if you don't know the answer. In these instances it is better to leave the answer blank.

Marking

Once you have completed the test you will be ready to mark it. The process to follow is simple:

- Go to *Non-verbal reasoning grid 2* (opposite) and complete this following the instructions on page 11.
- Transfer the total number of marks to the Summary box below and work out the percentage as directed.

Non-verbal reasoning test 2 summary

Total

Percentage

Work out your percentage using this sum

$\frac{\text{Total}}{34} \times 100 =$

4 Test for success

Non-verbal reasoning grid 2

Follow the instructions on page 11 to fill in this grid and page 12 for instructions for use.

Making connections

Question	Mark*	Skill	Page	To do	Try it out	Test yourself
1		Common connections	16			
2		Connections of direction, angle and symmetry	18			
3		Finding similarities and differences	20			
4						
5		Spotting distractions	22			
6						
Total	/6	Read 'Introducing making connections' first on pages 14–15 if you have missed any Skills in the Making connections section.				

Breaking codes

Question	Mark*	Skill	Page	To do	Try it out	Test yourself
7		Codes with two letters	26			
8						
9						
10		Codes with three letters	28			
11						
Total	/5	Read 'Introducing breaking codes' first on pages 24–25 if you have missed any Skills in the Breaking codes section.				

Finding relationships

Question	Mark*	Skill	Page	To do	Try it out	Test yourself
12		Changing shapes	32			
13						
14		Number and proportion	34			
15						
16		Moving and connecting shapes	36			
17						
18		Reflections in vertical lines**	38			
19		Reflections in horizontal and diagonal lines**	40			
20		Rotations**	42			
21						
Total	/10	Read 'Introducing finding relationships' first on pages 30–31 if you have missed any skills in the Finding relationships section.				

** If you find these skills challenging, try the extra practice questions in 'Working with reflections and rotations' on pages 68–69.

Spotting patterns

Question	Mark*	Skill	Page	To do	Try it out	Test yourself
22		More complex 2 × 2 grids	48			
23						
24						
25		More complex 3 × 3 grids	52			
26						
Total	/5	Read 'Introducing spotting patterns' first on pages 44–45 if you have missed any skills in the Spotting patterns section.				

Completing sequences

Question	Mark*	Skill	Page	To do	Try it out	Test yourself
27		Repeating patterns	56			
28						
29		One-step patterns	58			
30						
31		Two-step patterns	60			
32						
33		Simple number patterns	62			
34		Square and triangular number patterns	64			
Total	/8	Read 'Introducing completing sequences' first on pages 54–55 if you have missed any Skills in the Completing sequences section.				

*1 mark is allocated for each correct answer. There are no half marks.

Total /34 Add up your total for your Non-verbal reasoning test here.

4 Test for success

Now that you have your results from the second Practice test you can celebrate your success in areas where you have improved and plan for your final preparations.

Reviewing the final summary boxes

Look at your results in the Summary box on page 70 and review your scores. To be prepared for the 11+ tests you should be aiming to achieve results of 71% or higher in Non-verbal reasoning.

If you still have areas that need additional practice you can…

- look at the Non-verbal reasoning connections chart (opposite) which will show you skills that are commonly linked; if you are having difficulty with a particular type of question, look at the other pages that relate to it, and use the advice to help you
- revisit the relevant pages in the guide
- purchase additional materials linked to the specific skills you have identified in these tests.

If you are now achieving the suggested percentages, you should move on to take some 11+ Practice papers to boost your confidence and further develop your familiarity with the different question types you may encounter. These tests are also useful for increasing your speed in answering the questions.

Practice support

You may find the following Letts titles helpful for additional skills practice…

- Non-Verbal Reasoning Ages 9–10 Assessment Papers   9781844193356
- Non-Verbal Reasoning Ages 10–11 Assessment Papers   9781844193363
- More Non-Verbal Reasoning Ages 10–11 Assessment Papers 9781844195565

You may find the following Letts Practice papers helpful for your final preparations…

- 11+ Practice Papers Standard Non-Verbal Reasoning   9781844192427
- 11+ Practice Papers Multiple Choice Non-Verbal Reasoning 9781844192496

Note: you should buy the multiple-choice papers or the standard papers, but *not* both, as the content is the same.

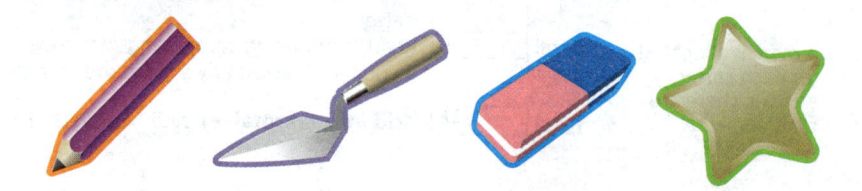

4 Test for success

This grid shows the connections between non-verbal reasoning skills.

If you are having difficulty with a certain type of question, the links here can direct you towards other areas to practise.

Page	Topic	Making connections	Common connections	Connections of direction, angle and symmetry	Finding similarities and differences	Spotting distractions	Breaking codes	Codes with two letters	Codes with three letters	Finding relationships	Changing shapes	Number and proportion	Moving and connecting shapes	Reflections in vertical lines	Reflections in horizontal and diagonal lines	Rotations	Spotting patterns	Simple 2 × 2 grids	More complex 2 × 2 grids	Simple 3 × 3 grids	More complex 3 × 3 grids	Completing sequences	Repeating patterns	One-step patterns	Two-step patterns	Simple number patterns	Square and triangular number patterns
		14	16	18	20	22	24	26	28	30	32	34	36	38	40	42	44	46	48	50	52	54	56	58	60	62	64
14	Making connections																										
16	Common connections		●	◆	◆	◆		◆	◆		◆	◆	◆	◆	◆	◆		◆	◆	◆	◆		◆	◆	◆	◆	◆
18	Connections of direction, angle and symmetry		◆	●	◆	◆		◆	◆		◆		◆			◆		◆	◆	◆	◆						
20	Finding similarities and differences		◆	◆	●	◆		◆	◆		◆	◆	◆	◆	◆	◆		◆			◆						
22	Spotting distractions		◆	◆	◆	●					◆	◆															
24	Breaking codes																										
26	Codes with two letters		◆	◆	◆	◆		●	◆		◆	◆	◆	◆	◆	◆											
28	Codes with three letters		◆	◆	◆			◆	●		◆	◆	◆	◆	◆	◆											
30	Finding relationships																										
32	Changing shapes		◆	◆	◆			◆	◆		●	◆	◆	◆	◆	◆		◆	◆	◆	◆		◆	◆	◆	◆	◆
34	Number and proportion		◆					◆	◆		◆	●														◆	◆
36	Moving and connecting shapes		◆	◆	◆			◆	◆		◆		●	◆	◆	◆		◆	◆	◆	◆		◆				
38	Reflections in vertical lines		◆		◆			◆	◆		◆		◆	●	◆			◆		◆			◆				
40	Reflections in horizontal and diagonal lines		◆		◆			◆	◆		◆		◆	◆	●			◆		◆			◆				
42	Rotations		◆	◆	◆			◆	◆		◆		◆			●		◆		◆			◆	◆	◆		
44	Spotting patterns																										
46	Simple 2 × 2 grids		◆	◆	◆						◆		◆					●	●								
48	More complex 2 × 2 grids		◆	◆	◆						◆		◆					●	●								
50	Simple 3 × 3 grids		◆	◆							◆		◆							●	●						
52	More complex 3 × 3 grids		◆	◆	◆	◆					◆		◆	◆	◆	◆				●	●						
54	Completing sequences																										
56	Repeating patterns		◆		◆						◆	◆	◆			◆							●	◆	◆	◆	
58	One-step patterns		◆		◆						◆	◆			◆	◆							◆	●			
60	Two-step patterns		◆		◆						◆	◆				◆							◆		●		
62	Simple number patterns		◆		◆						◆	◆											◆			●	
64	Square and triangular number patterns		◆		◆						◆	◆															●

◆ connecting skills   ● matching content pages

5 Show what you can do

Try following the steps given here to break your time down into easy-to-manage stages. This will help you feel much more in control and relaxed about your preparation.

Playing games in the weeks leading up to the tests helps you to become familiar with the skills you will need. You can share your preparation with your parents.

Spot the difference

Finding examples of 'spot the difference' activities in newspapers and magazines can help you improve your visual skills.

Making your own can be fun (you will need access to a photocopier to play this game).

- Draw a picture in pencil; photocopy your drawing.
- Add some extra parts to the original drawing and use an eraser to rub some out. Keep a count of how many alterations you make.
- Photocopy the new version. Have fun with friends, swapping pairs of drawings and seeing how many differences you and your friends can find.

Flag fun

Using just the primary colours of yellow, red and blue, how many different ways can you find to colour this flag design?

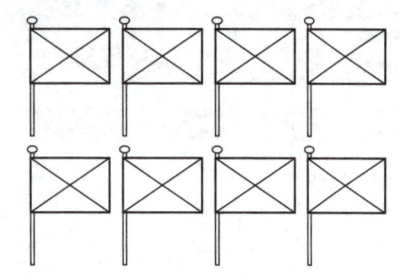

Bonus boxes

Play this game with a partner. You will need: a piece of dotted paper, two pencils or crayons in different colours.

The aim of the game is to make as many boxes as you can.

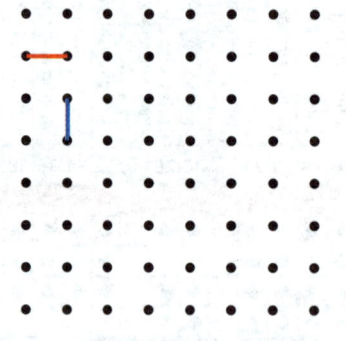

- The two players take turns to join the dots.
- When you make a box you get an extra turn. Write your initials in each box you complete.
- Try to stop your friend making boxes by colouring a line in your colour when it looks like they may be about to finish their box.
- The winner is the player who has the most boxes with their initials in at the end.

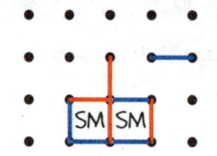

Perfect patterns

Try this activity on your own or with a friend. You will need: some card, sticky tape and a sheet of paper.

- Cut a regular shape from a piece of card.
- Cut a section from one side and use tape to join it to another side.

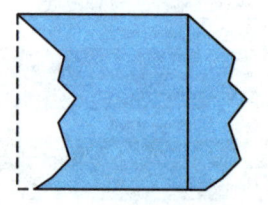

- If you draw the shape on the paper, you will see that you can join the card shape and the drawn shape together (they tessellate).
- You can now make new patterns by using the card as a template and colour in the patterns.

Finding ways that shapes tessellate will help you pick out patterns and rotations.

5 Show what you can do

Countdown to the tests

As soon as possible before the tests…

Check with the school you are applying to about their entrance requirements:

- Find out what exams your chosen school will be setting.
- Make sure you know the dates.

One week before the tests

- Check your travel arrangements and practise getting to the destination to make sure you know where to go.
- Make sure you have enough pens, pencils and an analogue watch so you can see how much time you have spent if you are timing your work.
- Check with the school if you need geometry equipment (ruler, set squares, protractor, compasses) if you are taking a Maths test and whether you can bring tracing paper and a mirror for the Maths and Non-verbal reasoning tests. Any equipment will need to be taken in a see-through pencil case.

During the week before the tests

- Allow yourself 90 minutes to check through any areas you're worried about up to two days before.
- Avoid last minute practice as this can make you anxious – do something with your friends or parents to help you relax the night before.
- Get a good night's sleep.

The day of the tests

- Eat a good breakfast.
- Leave in plenty of time, making allowances for traffic and other hold-ups.
- Take a healthy snack to boost your energy levels and a small bottle of water.
- Go to the toilet before you go in to the test.

During the tests

- Read the questions twice before you start writing.
- Make sure you understand what you are expected to do. For example, make sure you know how many selections you are being asked to make in multiple-choice questions and how you are supposed to mark down your answer.
- Underline key words in the questions.
- Make sure you know which questions get most marks. Spend your time accordingly.
- After half the time is up, check whether you have got to the stapled pages in the test. If you haven't, go through and do the easy questions in the second half of the paper.
- Even if you are in a hurry, make sure your work is easy to read.
- If you can't do a question, leave it. Come back to it at the end if you have time.
- Leave time at the end to check your work.

Non-verbal reasoning papers

- In some questions you will be asked to select the odd one out.
- In others you will be asked to find a group of images with something in common.
- Make sure that you are clear about what you are being asked to do.

If you need to write an answer in letters make sure that your writing is clear.

5 Show what you can do

Interview techniques

Many schools base their final selection on how well the applicants perform in an interview.

With the right preparation, you can use this opportunity to show your potential to be a good member of the school and find out whether this is the right place for you.

Discussion topics

Being prepared with interesting things to talk about during your interview is always a good idea.

If you have recently visited a museum, National Trust or English Heritage property these make ideal subjects to prepare for discussion. If you have taken part in a sporting event such as a rugby tournament or a cross-country run, these make equally good talking points.

Rather than writing down lots of information, take a small business card and create a spider diagram on the back. This diagram will remind you of the key points of interest that you can talk about, given the right opportunity by the interviewer.

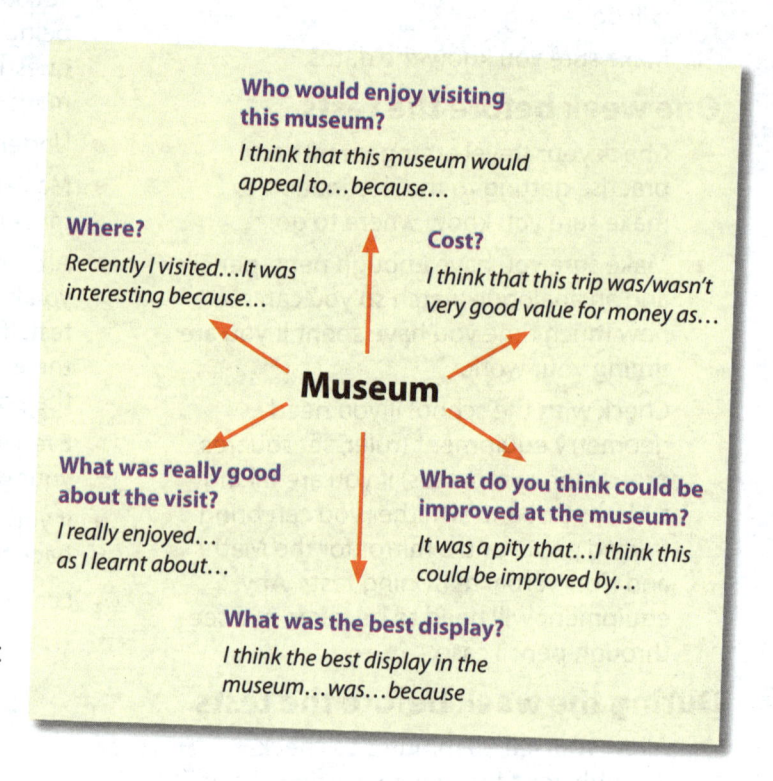

Who would enjoy visiting this museum?
I think that this museum would appeal to…because…

Where?
Recently I visited…It was interesting because…

Cost?
I think that this trip was/wasn't very good value for money as…

Museum

What was really good about the visit?
I really enjoyed… as I learnt about…

What do you think could be improved at the museum?
It was a pity that…I think this could be improved by…

What was the best display?
I think the best display in the museum…was…because

Meeting the interviewer
Waiting
- Calm yourself with the breathing techniques shown in the box, opposite.
- Do talk to other candidates who are waiting, but don't pester them for information.
- Read useful information on posters and notice boards in the room.

Entering the interview room
- Knock before you enter.
- Say 'hello' in a friendly and polite way.
- Shake hands firmly if the interviewer offers their hand.
- Wait for the interviewer to indicate a seat before you sit down.

RELAX

These techniques can help to calm your nerves when you are waiting to go into the interview room.

- Imagine you are holding an eggshell in each hand. This helps to relax your fingers and release tension.
- Breathe in slowly through your nose, counting to three and breathe out at the same pace. Concentrate on your breathing to clear your mind.

5 Show what you can do

Interview techniques

Body language
Basic body language
- Sit in a relaxed way, but don't slouch.
- Sit so that your body, including your legs and feet, points towards the interviewer.
- Don't put up barriers by crossing your arms in front of you.
- Smile, but only when appropriate – don't just grin all the time.

Hands
- Keep your hands away from your face and hair.
- Don't touch your nose before you answer a question.
- Use your hands to express yourself, but keep them on your lap at other times.

Eye contact
- Look at the interviewer, but don't stare – remember to blink.
- Don't be tempted to look away if they ask a difficult question.
- Don't shut your eyes while you think about a question.

Asking and answering questions
Avoiding yes/no answers
- Every question is an opportunity to tell the interviewer something about yourself.
- Don't just answer 'Yes' or 'No'. Give *positive* answers.

DRESS
First impressions are important. Find out in advance about what you should wear. Your current school uniform is usually a suitable option.
- Make sure that the clothes you are wearing are clean and ironed and that your shoes are clean.
- Make sure your hair is tidy and that your fringe isn't too long so that your eyes can be seen. If your hair is long, tie it back.

- Try adding an example to your answer, or qualify it ('No, but …', 'Yes, although I sometimes …').

Difficult questions
- If you're asked about an area of weakness, explain how you've tried to improve.
- If you're asked a factual question and don't know the answer, say so.
- If you don't understand a question, ask for it to be repeated or ask for an explanation.

Asking questions
- Prepare your own questions in advance.
- Don't ask questions you could easily find out the answers to.
- Ask a question that shows you have done some research about the school and would like to find out more.

Ending the interview
Thanking the interviewer
- Thank the interviewer for their time.
- Add something like, 'I've enjoyed talking with you.'

Saying goodbye
- Respond with a firm handshake if the interviewer offers their hand.
- Close the door quietly when you leave.

QUESTIONS
Think about questions you could ask at the end of your interview. They could be questions about the school in general or about specific subjects or sports that interest you. Here are some examples:
- What is special about your secondary school that is different from the other schools in the area?
- What are the most popular universities students choose when leaving the school?
- I really enjoy rugby. Are there opportunities to take part in inter-school competitions?

77

5 Show what you can do

After the tests

Once you have taken the tests, the marking and admissions process begins.

Although you'll need to wait to hear if you have been given a place at the school, you can spend some of the time finding out about what happens next.

Waiting for results

Results for the 11+ tests do not come quickly and you should expect to wait between 10 and 16 weeks. If the school you have applied to has not already told you when the results will be available, ask a parent to check the date with the school or the Local Education Authority (LEA).

Understanding the results

The pass mark

The pass mark can change from year to year as it is based on how many places there are at the school. You may also find that the pass mark for boys and girls is different – this happens when a school wants to balance the number of students from each sex in the year group.

Standardisation

In order to make the testing process fair, scores are *standardised* by age. This means that if you are one of the younger children in your age group, the school will take this into account when deciding your final marks.

When the results are not as you expect

Offers from LEA schools

If you have applied to an LEA school, you will have been offered a choice of up to three schools.

If you don't get into your first choice of school, your name will be placed on the list for your second choice. Although the schools generally take students who have put them down first on the list, there are sometimes a few spare places. If your second choice of school is full then you will be passed on to your third choice, so don't give up hope!

Offers from private and independent schools

If you have applied to a private or independent school you will not be offered an alternative school unless you have applied to these separately and taken their 11+ tests as well.

What to do if you don't agree with the result

If you haven't been lucky enough to get a place at your chosen school, your family have a right to find out why. It may be that your test results were the reason for being turned down but there could also be other reasons such as the distance you live from the school.

When you have found out the reasons but you're not happy with what you have been told, your family can put in an 'appeal' (if it is a local authority school) to see if you can get the decision changed.

Although appeals are usually carried out in a friendly way, the process is quite formal. There are a number of organisations that can help with advice, including the Advisory Centre for Education (ACE). There is also a wide selection of private companies who specialise in supporting families in putting appeals forward.

Test answers

Making connections

Common connections 17

1 **e**: triangle e is made up of dashed lines. The other triangles are made up of solid lines.
2 **e**: shape e is a rectangle. The other shapes are all squares of differing sizes.

Connections of direction, angle and symmetry 19

1 **c**: arrow c matches the two arrow on the left because it has an identical arrow head. All the other arrows have different styles of arrow head.
2 **e**: triangle e matches the two triangles on the left because it is also an isosceles triangle.

Finding similarities and differences 21

1 **c**: shape c matches the two shapes on the left because it is also a white square made up of solid lines.
2 **a**: the image in box a matches the two images in the boxes on the left because it also has two black segments and two spotted segments.

Spotting distractions 23

e: image e matches the two images on the left because it also has an alternating colour pattern (black squares follow white squares and white squares follow black squares). The arrow is a distraction.

Breaking codes

Codes with two letters 27

b: A, C and B are the codes for the colour. M, L and N are the codes for the number of small squares. The fifth shape is grey (C) and has three small squares (M). The answer is CM.

Codes with three letters 29

d: D and E are the codes for the direction of the diagonal strip. H, I and J are the codes for the shape of the top of the shield. X, Y and Z are the codes for the shading of the shield.

The fifth shape has a diagonal strip that goes from top left to bottom right (E), the shield has three points at the top (I) and the shield is vertically striped (X). The answer is EIX.

Finding relationships

Changing shapes 33

1 **c**: the images in the boxes swap sizes and positions. There are no changes to the shading.
2 **b**: squares become circles, circles become triangles and triangles become squares. Black shapes become white, white shapes become striped and striped shapes become black.

Number and proportion 35

1 **b**: the shapes in image b have a total of nine corners. This matches the number of corners in two images on the left.
2 **e**: image e also has three of its eight segments shaded in.

Moving and connecting shapes 37

1 **e**: the two small shapes move outside of the larger shape. The larger shape does not move.
2 **b**: the black shape slides up over the white shape until the patterns match up (join together).

Reflections in vertical lines 39

1 **b**: the shape in the box is reflected in a vertical mirror line.
2 **c**: in the first pair of images the car body and roof are shaded black and the whole image is reflected in a vertical mirror line. In image c both the body and sail of the boat have been shaded black and reflected in a vertical mirror line.

Reflections in horizontal and diagonal lines 41

1 **e**: the image in the box is reflected in a horizontal mirror line.
2 **d**: the image in the box is reflected in a diagonal mirror line going from the bottom left to the top right.

Rotations 43

a: the outer segments in each box rotate 90° clockwise while the inner segments rotate 45° anticlockwise.

Improve your skills answers

79

Test answers

Spotting patterns

Simple 2 × 2 grids   47

b: moving across from left to right, the shape in each box gets smaller and the shading goes from black to white.

More complex 2 × 2 grids   49

1 **b**: the images in each box are reflected in a horizontal mirror line. The images at the bottom of the grid are a reflection of the images at the top.

2 **d**: moving across from left to right the white images in the boxes pick up an alternating black and white pattern. In the black and white image, the top segment of the outer shape is white, the segments then alternate between black and white. The top segment on the inner shape is black and the segments then alternate between white and black.

Simple 3 × 3 grids   51

a: as the shapes in the boxes move down to the next row in each column they get smaller. The shapes are reflected in a horizontal mirror line (or rotated 180°) as they move down a row.

More complex 3 × 3 grids   53

1 **e**: the top row contains three different images. As you go down to the next row the images move one box along to the right. The images are also rotated 90° anticlockwise.

2 **c**: the first column of boxes is reflected in a vertical mirror line to make the last column of boxes and the shapes within them swap colours.

Completing sequences

Repeating patterns   57

1 **b**: the triangle rotates 180° each time and alternates between black and white.

2 **d**: one of the circles is removed and a triangle is added in each box as the pattern moves from left to right. All the shapes alternate between black and white with each step.

One-step patterns   59

e: the black circle moves one place around the star each time in a clockwise direction, stopping between the points.

Two-step patterns   61

d: there are two patterns in this sequence. The first happens with every step – the image is reflected in a horizontal mirror line each time. The second happens with every other step – the black circle moves to the next point of the small black triangle in an anticlockwise direction in every other box.

Simple number patterns   63

1 **d**: the number of triangles increases by three in each box as the pattern moves from left to right.

2 **b**: the number of circles decreases by two in each box as the pattern moves from left to right.

Square and triangular number patterns   65

c: the number of items in each box matches the sequence of triangular numbers.

80

Test answers

Working with reflections and rotations

Reflective symmetry with one mirror line — 68

Reflections in vertical lines

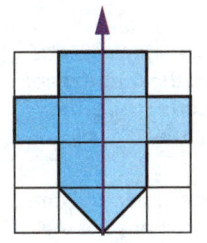

Reflections in horizontal lines

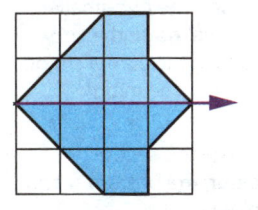

Reflections in diagonal lines

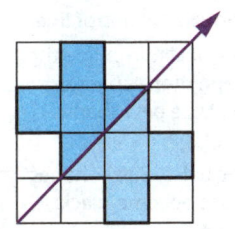

Reflective symmetry with two mirror lines — 68

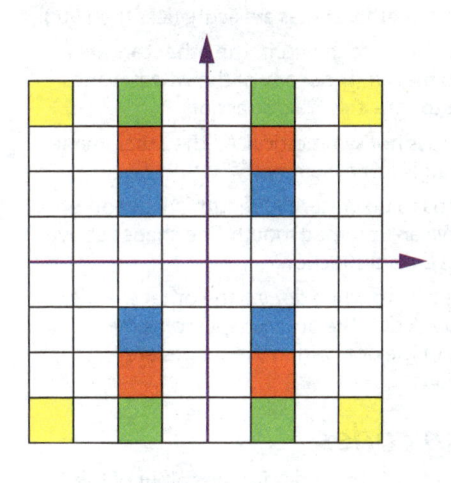

Reflections in two diagonal lines — 69

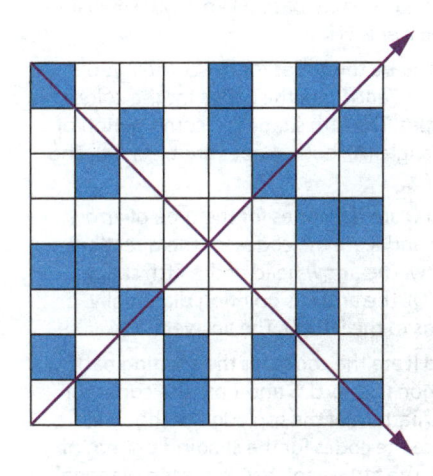

Rotations — 69

7 heptagon

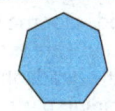

1 L and trapezium

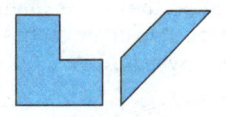

4 cross

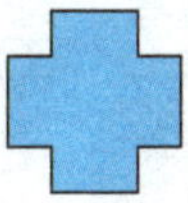

Test answers

Making connections

1. **c**: triangle c is black. All the other triangles are white.
2. **d**: angle d is obtuse (greater than 90° and less than 180°). All the other angles are acute (less than 90°).
3. **e**: car e is facing to the right. The other cars are facing to the left. The shape of the wheels varies from car to car – this is a distraction.
4. **a**: image a is not symmetrical. All the other images have a single line of symmetry.
5. **c**: face c has a down-turned mouth. All the other faces have an upturned mouth. The shapes above the faces are a distraction.
6. **b**: shape b has a white dot. All the other shapes have a black dot. The outer shapes, plus the position of the dots within the shapes are distractions.

Breaking codes

7. **e**: C, D and E are the codes for the colour of the base. F, H and G are the codes for the number of small lines branching off the tall vertical line. The fifth shape has a white base (E) and four small lines (H). The answer is EH.
8. **b**: C, B and A are the codes for the combination of shapes. Y, X and Z are the codes for the colour of the shapes. The fifth shape is a combination of square/triangle (A); both shapes are black (X). The answer is AX.
9. **b**: P, O and Q are the codes for the type of arrow head. W, V and X are the codes for the direction of the arrow. The arrow head of the fifth shape is a circle (Q); the arrow is pointing diagonally downwards to the left (X). The answer is QX.
10. **d**: Q, P and R are the codes for the shading pattern of the diagonal strip. U, S and T are the codes for the shape/pattern of the top edge of the shield. X, V and W are the codes for the shading pattern of the shield. The fifth shape has a spotted diagonal strip (R) and is a shield with a curved edge (S); the shield has a striped pattern (X). The answer is RSX.
11. **e**: B and A are the codes for the position of the steering wheel. I, H and J are the codes for the shading pattern of the headlights. U, W and V are the codes for the shading pattern of the top strip. The steering wheel in the fifth shape is positioned to the left (A); the car has spotted headlights (H) and the top strip of the car has diagonal stripes (W). The answer is AHW.

Finding relationships

12. **b**: the image is rotated 90°. The centre shape becomes black and the middle section of the corner pattern becomes black.
13. **b**: the image is rotated 90° and reduced in size. Black stripes become white and white stripes become black.
14. **d**: the outer shape increases in size and the centre shape decreases in size. Copies of the centre shape appear in all the corners of the outer shape. The copies are the opposite colour to the original centre shape.
15. **e**: two copies of the original shape appear. All three shapes overlap with one shape positioned at the top and two shapes at the bottom.
16. **e**: the small shape moves from the bottom right corner to the bottom left corner. The two smaller versions of the large shape move inside the large shape; these shapes move above the corner shape to the right. The smallest shape in the middle becomes black.
17. **a**: the image is rotated 180°. The top section changes to the opposite colour; the bottom section changes to the opposite colour.
18. **a**: the second image is reflected in a vertical mirror line.
19. **c**: the image is reflected in a horizontal mirror line.
20. **e**: the shape is reflected in a vertical mirror line then rotated 90° clockwise. The shape then separates to form two new shapes; one of the new shapes is a rectangle.
21. **a**: the image is rotated 90° clockwise. Black shapes become white and white shapes become black.

Spotting patterns

22. **a**: moving from left to right, the inner and outer shapes in each box increase in size. A third white shape appears in the centre of the inner shape.
23. **b**: moving from left to right, the top shapes in each box are stretched. The top line (made up of four identical segments) becomes a straight line, with one segment of the original line positioned centrally below it.
24. **a**: the images in each box are reflected in a vertical mirror line. As the images move from one box to the next (not diagonally), black shapes become white; white shapes become black. Diagonal squares have the same colour pattern.
25. **d**: as the shapes move down a row, they increase in size and move one box to the right.
26. **a**: the images in the top row of boxes are reflected in a horizontal mirror line to make the bottom row of boxes. The whole pattern is symmetrical if you put a horizontal mirror line across the centre.

Test answers

Test 1 answers

Completing sequences

27 d: this repeating pattern starts at one circle then increases by one circle each time; when there are three circles the pattern decreases by one circle each time. The smaller circles are always positioned inside the large circle, at the bottom.

28 e: the shading moves out to the next circle each time. When it reaches the outer circle, it goes back to the centre and the pattern is repeated.

29 b: the number of lines (sides) increases by one each time; there is a circle at each point; the circles are always positioned under the shapes.

30 a: the black shading goes anticlockwise around the shape and moves round two circles at a time.

31 e: there are two separate patterns in this sequence. The first pattern is the sequence of small circles which appear in the top left-hand corner of every other box. The small circles increase by one each time and have an alternating colour pattern; black circles change to white and white circles change to black with each step. The second pattern is the sequence of larger circles. These increase by one each time; black circles change to white and white circles change to black with each step.

32 a: there are two separate patterns in this sequence. The first pattern is the sequence of curved lines which appear in the bottom left-hand corner of every other box. These decrease by two each time. The second pattern is the sequence of zig-zag lines; these increase by one inverted 'V' shape each time.

33 b: this sequence increases and decreases in multiples of three. The pattern starts at three; when in reaches nine it decreases until it reaches three again. The variation of shapes is a distraction.

34 a: the small circles positioned in the centre increase by one each time; the corner lines increase by two.

Test 2 answers

Making connections

1 a: image a matches the two images on the left because it is also made up of equilateral triangles (equilateral triangles have equal angles and sides of equal length).

2 d: image d matches the two images on the left because the small lines branching off the tall vertical line are also pointing upwards.

3 b: image b matches the two images on the left because it also has one small shape in each corner.

4 c: image c matches the two images on the left because it also has a total of one quarter of each particular shading type.

5 b: image b matches the two images on the left because it is also a shield with two parallel lines near the flat end and an unshaded shape at the other end. The circle on the edge of some of the shields is a distraction.

6 e: image e matches the two images on the left because it is also an irregular hexagon with four squares and one rectangle, all arranged to look like a house. The shaded 'door' and 'chimney pot' are distractions.

Breaking codes

7 d: L, M and N are the codes for the hair length. W, V and U are the codes for the direction of the mouth. The fifth image (face) has long hair (M) and an upturned mouth (U). The answer is MU.

8 b: A, C and B are the codes for the shading pattern of the pairs of segments that are horizontally (left/right) and vertically (top/bottom) opposite. E, F and D are the codes for the shading pattern of the pairs of segments that are diagonally opposite. The segments that are vertically and horizontally opposite in the fifth image are spotted (C); the segments diagonally opposite are striped (D). The answer is CD.

9 d: I, H and G are the codes for the shading pattern. K, L and M are the codes for the number of corners. The fifth shape has a diagonal pattern (I) and seven corners (M). The answer is IM.

10 e: G, F and E are the codes for the completed image. C, A and B are the codes for the size of the shape. I, J and K are the codes for the shading pattern of the shape. The fifth shape is a circle (E) and is medium-sized (B); the circle has a diagonal shading pattern – the diagonal lines go from top left to bottom right (I). The arrow is a distraction. The answer is EBI.

11 a: Q, R and S are the codes for the direction of the strip inside the shield. A, C and B are the codes for the shading pattern of the shield. L, K and I are the codes for the shading pattern of the strip. The fifth shape has a diagonal strip going from top left to bottom right (S); the shield is white (C) and the strip has a striped pattern (K). The answer is SCK.

83

Test answers

Finding relationships

12 **a**: the second shape is a solid 3-D version of the first.
13 **b**: black shapes become white, striped shapes become black and white shapes become striped.
14 **a**: the number of small shapes are doubled. Circles remain circles and squares remain squares.
15 **c**: the outer shape reduces in size and moves down and to the right to fit over the smaller version of the outer shape. The shape that differs from the other two moves outside the large shape. Two copies of this shape appear; the shapes do not change direction.
16 **e**: the sections are joined together. The complete image is reflected in a vertical mirror line, then rotated 45° anticlockwise.
17 **b**: the two separate shapes are slotted together to make a whole shape.
18 **a**: the shape is reflected in a vertical mirror line and black becomes white.
19 **a**: the image is are reflected in a diagonal mirror line.
20 **b**: the image is rotated 180°.
21 **a**: the image is rotated 135° clockwise.

Spotting patterns

22 **a**: the images in the boxes are reflected in a vertical mirror line. The shapes in the left-hand boxes have no colour, shading or pattern.
23 **c**: moving from top to bottom, the images are rotated 90° clockwise.
24 **b**: the images move down and to the left. The shading patterns move down and to the right.
25 **c**: as the images move down a row they rotate 90° anticlockwise and move one box to the right.
26 **b**: as the images move down a row they rotate 90° anticlockwise and move one box to the left.

Completing sequences

27 **e**: the triangle alternates between spotted and white. The right-angled triangle rotates 90° clockwise. The rectangle moves anticlockwise around the outside of the triangle.
28 **c**: the small square in the centre alternates between black and white. The middle square has four sections. The right-hand section of the middle square is always shaded with a diagonal pattern from bottom left to top right. There is another shaded section which has a diagonal pattern from top left to bottom right. This rotates 90° clockwise. When the two shaded sections overlap there is a diamond pattern. The outer square starts white; it is then shaded black, one segment at a time in an anticlockwise direction.
29 **e**: the image rotates 135° anticlockwise.
30 **b**: the lines in the top right-hand corner decrease by one each time. The shape in the centre is a distraction.
31 **e**: the shading in the outer segments rotates two segments clockwise, while the shading in the inner segments rotates one segment anticlockwise.
32 **a**: each box has a total of six shapes in it. In every second box the number of squares decreases by one and a triangle is added. In the intervening boxes one of the triangles becomes a circle.
33 **c**: the number of stars corresponds to the sequence of triangular numbers, 1, 3, 6, 10, 15… A line is added each time to the corner in an anticlockwise direction.
34 **c**: the lines are arranged to look like a house: the rule is 'add 3 lines'.